STRONGER MAN NATION
Biblical Manhood Series

SON
SET FREE TO LOVE

Adam James

GRACE CITY
PUBLISHING
WENATCHEE, WA

GRACE CITY
PUBLISHING
WENATCHEE, WA

To my sons—Benjamin and Samuel—with whom I am well pleased, and my dad—Larry James—whom I honor. Dad, thank you for making the Word of God the foundation of your life and putting it in mine.

To Greg McPherson, Kent McMullen, and Phil Rogers, spiritual fathers to many, including me. You have impacted my life and ministry beyond words.

To Josh McPherson, the greatest leader and friend I've had the privilege of riding the trail with all these years. Thank you for leading.

To my wife, Erin, you've made me a better son, father, husband, and man.

You then, my **SON,** be strong in the grace that is in Christ Jesus. And the things you have heard me say in the presence of many witnesses entrust to reliable men who will also be qualified to teach others. Join with me in suffering, like a good **SOLDIER** of Christ Jesus. No one serving as a soldier gets entangled in civilian affairs, but rather tries to please his commanding officer. Similarly, anyone who competes as an **ATHLETE** does not receive the victor's crown except by competing according to the rules. The hardworking **FARMER** should be the first to receive a share of the crops. Reflect on what I am saying, for the Lord will give you insight into all this.

2 TIMOTHY 2:1-7

STRONGER MAN NATION

is a movement of like-minded men.

We're living out biblical manhood
with clear eyes in a confused culture.

We're committed to making good battle
with our lives. We follow the Stronger Man
— Jesus Christ —
and we'd love for you to join us.

→ Annual conference on Father's Day weekend.

→ Monthly rallies.

→ Project ManCard Rite-of-Passage Experiences
for fathers and sons.

→ Helpful resources.

WWW.STRONGERMANNATION.COM

CONTENTS

ACKNOWLEDGMENTS

To the tribe of Stronger Man Nation, and the men who join me each first Wednesday of the month at 0600 to fan the flame of true manhood, thank you for your passion and hunger that is inspiring so many other men, including me. To the family of Grace City Church, thank you for your faithfulness and generosity that made this project possible. To Pastor Josh, thank you for your vision and desire to free me up to produce content for men and for our church family—it is an incredible blessing. To my fellow elders, Kent and Kyle, thank you for modeling these truths and supporting this endeavor. Thank you to the many friends who intentionally prayed for me during the writing retreats and encouraged me with texts along the way. Thank you to the Stronger Men who shared their testimonies and experiences for each chapter; your stories put skin on the reality of the power and impact of fathers. Thank you, again, specifically, to the tireless Karis McPherson and all her designing and formatting to craft a visually and aesthetically pleasing and accessible resource. To the man, the myth, the legend, Luke Ellington, who quarterbacks timelines, editing, printing, and production—and whose genuine excitement for these tools is motivating and inspiring. To Adam Ross, for your encouragement and help with the questions and actions, and for being an occasional, verbal-processing sounding board to flesh out ideas and insights. To the group of men I meet with Friday mornings at 5:30am, and all the men I've circled up with in various seasons over the years, thanks for digging in and working it out in real time. Thank you to the generous folks who have provided spaces for me to think, pray, and write—space matters, and yours were gifts. To my incredibly helpful and supportive wife, Erin, thank you for your encouragement, for joining me on the writing retreats, for reading every word, and for your attention to detail in the editing process. You know me best.

FOREWORD

Welcome to Stronger Man Nation. A way of life for the bold.

The book you are holding will make you a Stronger Man.

I say this with great confidence, mainly because the man who wrote it has pushed me to be a Stronger Man for twenty-five years.

I first met Adam in college. I was a straitlaced, homeschooled kid naive to the ways of the world, Adam a swaggering punk on the basketball team living for the next big party. Not a likely pair.

But Jesus is in the habit of converging the roads of unlikely friends and forging between them deep bonds of camaraderie and brotherhood. And so He did.

Since then, we've spent the better part of a quarter century shoulder-to-shoulder in the trenches working, sweating, dreaming, laughing, and all-around making merry battle on the fields of full-time ministry. It has been, for me, a life-changing friendship.

I say life-changing because when you get anywhere near the Adam James orbit, you encounter a white-hot nuclear reactor pulsing with spiritual passion. Adam's affection for Jesus is contagious. If you don't have a fire for Jesus, he'll start one. If you've got one, he'll stoke it hot. It's just the James way.

Which is why, one cold, winter afternoon, I walked out to his job trailer with an idea for the men of our church. I wanted Adam to crack the door of his soul-furnace and expose them to the blast of heat that emanates from a heart on fire for God's glory.

When I asked him if he would write a resource for men built around the four cornerstone identities of Stronger Man Nation, it was not only because I thought him a good writer, which he is. I asked him because Adam is a good man. And more importantly, he's good at being a man.

And we desperately need more good men good at being men.

Why? Well, allow me to speak plainly. The days are evil, men are wimps, and the enemy is playing for keeps.

Let's break that down.

The days are evil. As I write, it's legal in my town for the state to shuttle a child to a "gender therapy" center and begin irreversible hormonal castration or surgical mutilation (whichever the 14-year-old and their state-assigned counselor deem most beneficial for the child's mental health).

And all of this can be done without a parent's knowledge or permission.

But that same kid couldn't go to a tanning salon without parental consent, because the same state that hides gender reassignment "therapy" from parents has deemed getting a tan potentially too harmful for a child's health to attempt without parental permission.

As you can see, not only are the days abhorrently evil, they are absurdly bizarre.

Men are wimps. Okay, let me qualify that. Not every man is a wimp. Just too many of them. The masculinity crisis of our day is well documented. Men are on the run, chased into the shadows by a cancel culture built to swarm any man who dares show a hint of brawny moral backbone.

It's not so much that men have lost their way—they have lost their proverbial nerve. It's not that being a Stronger Man is a mystery, it's that being a Stronger Man takes guts. And guts, these days, are in short supply.

Thankfully, this is not true of the men and sons who make up Stronger Man Nation. May their tribe increase.

The enemy is playing for keeps. Here's some more plain speak...the enemy has your number and he's coming for you full throttle. War is upon us and the bullets are real. The cost for a lack of vigilance is steep. The enemy has breached the gate.

It's time that we, as Christian men, circle the wagons, grow a pair, and mount a counter-offensive. It's time we stop looking for the path of least resistance and start picking the biggest enemy target we can find and charging it with a whoop and a holler.

It's time we flip the script. No longer is the enemy hunting us—we are hunting him. And we have a bone to pick. "The gates of Hell will not prevail..." assumes an offensive posture of God's men. It's time to live like it.

If any of that resonates in your heart, this devotional book is for you. It will help you become that kind of man—a man who learns how to submit to the Lordship of Jesus Christ, and in so doing, becomes dangerous to the kingdom of darkness.

I am deeply grateful that these original devotionals, which Adam wrote for the men of our house, are now being made available to a wider audience in this power-packed, four-part series. I have witnessed, firsthand, the fire it has stoked in hundreds and hundreds of men in our local church. I pray it does the same for you.

God is writing a divine story of glory for your life. Don't miss it. The pages of these books will help you see that story, and more importantly, show you how to step into it with gumption. This isn't just a book to read; it's a playbook to live. There is an immediacy to its application. It's a field guide for how to start being a Stronger Man today.

However this book got into your hands, consider it the grace of God. He must love you (maybe more than you thought) and have good battle for you to make in the days and weeks ahead. Thrilling.

So grab some dudes, get a time on the calendar, and get after it. Time is ticking, the war is raging, and we need more fierce warriors happily slaying dragons with zeal and prejudice.

I look forward to seeing you on the field of battle.

Pastor Josh McPherson
Founder, Stronger Man Nation
Lead Pastor, Grace City Church

INTRODUCTION

What does it mean to be a man?

It's one of the most vital questions men ask.

To say we are witnessing an identity crisis (on a national level, at least) is an understatement. What is a man? What is a woman? Who or what determines our identity? Is it culture? Feelings? Tradition? Biology?

Let's be crystal clear, God determines your identity. "*Male and female He created them*" (**Genesis 1:27**). Your created biological identity is the objective starting point for your sexuality and gender. And that's a good thing.

To every man reading this, young or old: God made you a man ⇢ Sin made you a slave ⇢ God's grace through Jesus Christ can make you a loved son.

The most important and powerful earthly relationship we have is with our father. Our father is, by his God-given station and role, the first representative of God in our lives. That can be helpful, terrible, or confusing, depending on the character and impact of your dad in your life.

No man can truly fill those shoes. Every father is a broken, sinful man. Which means, he is also a broken image of what a father should be. Through the transforming power of God's grace, a man can become a loving father, a good example, and a window into the true character of God the Father, but he will never be able to meet the deepest needs of the masculine soul. For blessing. For affirmation. For approval. For protection and provision. For leadership.

God created "family." And God created "fathers." God designed men to be fathers and to bear the responsibility of that role and image. Thus the impact of fatherhood, or the lack of fatherhood, is the single greatest contributing factor to human relational development. It's undeniable because it is God's created design. The research has been proven over and over again. The statistics are dramatic. You can readily find them. The presence or absence of a father is the single greatest determining factor in social well-being and all manner of societal ills.

God Himself is the Father of all fatherhood. By that I do not mean He is the author of destructive and broken fatherhood. Sin has destroyed and marred the image of "father" for humanity in countless ways. But as author and pastor Louie Giglio says, "God is not the reflection of your earthly father. He's the perfection of everything your earthly father should have been."

In other words, whatever your experience with your own dad, God is not just a blown up version of your earthly father. God is everything a good father should be and everything a bad father isn't. And so much more.

For a man to come to know God as his true, heavenly Father, and to be welcomed, loved, embraced, blessed, armed, and empowered, is the highest and greatest blessing in life. The power of the gospel is not just that our sins can be forgiven through Jesus Christ but that we are given access to the Father, welcomed back into the family, given a seat at the table, and called "son."

To hear the words, "This is my son, with whom I am well pleased," which God the Father spoke to Jesus Christ at His baptism, is the most liberating truth of the gospel. Through faith in Christ, we are invited into that blessing, with Christ as our true older brother and the firstborn Son among many.

The deepest root of our identity as sons comes through our knowledge and experience of spiritual adoption as sons of our heavenly Father through faith in Jesus Christ. We are born as slaves of sin and only made free sons of God by the powerful, life-changing grace of God.

That's explosive good news. Liberating truth. Healing reality.

Regardless of the kind of dad you had, you can become a whole, strong, confident, loved, fully-free man.

Throughout this 4-part Biblical Manhood Series, we are looking at the primary images God has given in His Word that make up what it means to be a man. Right from the pages of 2 Timothy chapter 2, as the Apostle Paul is passing the baton to his spiritual son, Timothy. Paul calls Timothy to be a Stronger Man. He calls him to protect, provide, lead, and love like a soldier, farmer, athlete, and son.

Timothy didn't have a godly, earthly father. His sincere faith was modeled to him first by his grandmother, Lois, and then by his mother, Eunice. Where fathers are absent, by all means, we praise God for godly, strong, noble women of faith. Yes and amen. There's been more than a few praying grandmothers and mothers who have sought the Lord on their children's behalf, have passed the faith on to the next generation, and have prayed down blessings on their children.

But Timothy still needed a Stronger Man father-figure to enter the picture and help him grow in ways only the influence of another man can bring into a boy's life. For Timothy, that was the Apostle Paul. Paul became a spiritual father to Timothy. There are two books in the New Testament that bear Timothy's name: letters written by Paul that reveal the relationship that God used to build Timothy up as a Stronger Man.

"*To Timothy, my true son in the faith...*" (**1 Timothy 1:2**).

"*To Timothy, my dear son...*" (**2 Timothy 1:2**).

Paul helped guide Timothy into mature, stronger manhood. He showed him the power, freedom, confidence, and grace that are present in the gospel to fill the void left by an absent, apathetic, harsh, or unbelieving dad.

As we look at the images of soldier, farmer, and athlete, we see the toughness latent in what it means to be a man. But the image isn't complete without the tender side of manhood.

A Stronger Man is a man who loves deeply. He is a man who understands how to give and receive grace. He can throw himself at any threat, and he can comfort his wife and children.

He can charge the hill, plow the field, run the race, and raise his hands in worship while shedding tears of gratitude and praise to his heavenly Father as he leads his family and friends into a life of full dependence and trust in God.

Men are made and called to protect, provide, lead, and love as soldiers, farmers, athletes, and sons. We are warriors, workers, winners, and worshippers.

The Biblical Manhood Series is all about helping men become and build those kinds of men so we can bless women, children, the Church, and the world.

The world needs Stronger Men. The world needs godly fathers. The world needs loved sons who live to please their heavenly Father.

Without all four images and roles being embraced and embodied, our masculinity is muted and our soul less than mature and less than free.

Stronger Men listen, think, laugh, sing, confess sin, purge weakness, and display compassion and love to those they protect, provide for, and lead.

We are men who can wrestle on the floor, act silly, tell good stories, read aloud, give appropriate hugs and physical expressions of comfort, offer words of affection and affirmation, make eye contact, and listen carefully from the heart.

We are men who are both dangerous and safe. Dangerous to the enemy and safe for our families.

Stronger Men are set free to love. They are lovers of God with a heavenly Father to live for, a noble woman to win, and, Lord willing, sons and daughters to raise to carry on the legacy of faith for generations to come.

Brothers, let's step fully into our blood-bought sonship in the family of God and live in the powerful freedom of stronger manhood.

That is what we will explore and unpack together in the coming chapters.

Additionally, in each chapter, you'll hear a real testimony and story from a fellow Stronger Man. Their stories cover a range of experiences. From exemplary dads to broken homes to powerful redemption stories to stories still in progress. All of them point us to the freedom and power of knowing God as our Father.

Before we dive in, here's a snapshot of my own story.

MY STORY

I'm the youngest of three sons, and my parents are both first generation followers of Jesus. My dad and mom both gave their lives to Jesus the year before I was born, for which I am profoundly grateful. I grew up in a very small, very rural town in central Washington State. There were very few options for church and my parents did their best to learn and grow in their faith, while raising their young family and running a small business. It was not uncommon for my dad to work 80-hour weeks running the store. He was often gone before I got up and came home after I was in bed. I know he carries some regret over the hours he worked and the things he didn't know about raising sons. But let me be clear: It's easy for me to love and honor my dad.

My dad put the Word of God in my mind and heart, put a roof over my head, clothes on my back, gave me birthday parties and Christmas presents, took me camping, took us on memorable vacations, always made time to celebrate the holidays together, and he was in the stands at all my games. He served faithfully for decades in small, challenging church settings. He's seen the underbelly of the Church, and remained faithful to Jesus, because his faith is genuine. He has handled his finances with integrity and wisdom, and he's stayed faithful to my mom for over 50 years. My dad is a Stronger Man. And he's still growing and learning today.

Growing up, our family van became the church van. We'd pick up elderly folks or kids who needed a ride and take them 11 miles up the winding road, alongside the Methow River in North Central WA, to hear about Jesus. My parents eventually taught kids in Sunday school, complete with flannel graphs and learning songs and rhymes, to help kids learn the books of the Bible and sing the truth that "Jesus Loves Me."

My dad even stepped in to preach and fill the pulpit in our little country church when the pastor, who had been in the community for 30+ years, was arrested and ended up going to prison as a convicted child molester. The news broke when I was in the 6th grade. At that moment, my sinful heart didn't want to be associated with "church" or "God." Thankfully, neither my brothers nor I were victims of that evil man's actions, but the fallout of his sin certainly impacted our view of Christianity and the Church. My dad stepped in to teach that little band of believers for 10 weeks until an interim pastor could be secured. He pointed them to the truth about God, not about a broken man. I'm proud of my dad for being a man who anchored his faith not in the words of men but in the Word of God.

Today, he attends the church I help pastor, serves regularly, and sits under my preaching, telling me how proud he is of me. He supports my wife and me and his grandkids as we manage a full life with an active, growing church. His presence in our lives is a great blessing.

As I reflect on my story and my sinful rebellion, through my high school and early college years, it's less about my dad's failures or weaknesses and more about my own sinful, rebellious heart. Earlier in my life, I almost let the enemy convince me that I was a victim of a bad dad. It's so easy to take up the victim card and play the poor me attitude. But I had to face my own sin and sinful choices for what they were: MINE. No one made me lie. I did that. No one made me experiment with drugs. I did that. No one made me seek the attention and approval of peers. My sinful heart craved self-seeking glory. The humbling truth that is clearer by the day is simply this: I wasn't a good son.

Even though I had a dad who was trying his best with what he knew, I still needed a better Father. Just like he did too. Just like we all do. I needed the grace of Jesus to transform my sinful heart and show me the way to the Father whose love would wash over me and set me on a whole new course of what it means to know I'm a loved son.

WEEK 1

STRONGER MEN LIVE LIKE SONS

You then my **SON** be strong in the grace that is in Christ Jesus.

2 TIMOTHY 2:1

A stronger man is a man who finds his strength in the grace of Jesus.

This is a curveball for most men.

We don't usually associate the word "strong" with the word "grace."

We usually associate grace as feminine or weakness. That's why Grace is used as a girl's name. My wife and I named our oldest daughter Grace.

But true, biblical grace is anything but weak. It's explosive. It's powerful. It's transformative. It is by grace alone that men are saved, changed, built, and rebuilt.

What is grace? It's the unearned, undeserved, favor of God. Grace is God's generous love in action. It's the gift of God.

It's the only thing that can make you a truly Stronger Man.

Men need blunt and direct communication, so here you go: if you don't understand and receive God's grace through Christ Jesus, you'll actually remain some version of a weak, insecure, orphan-minded, hardhearted, arrogant, ignorant, passive, or abusive boy. Not a Stronger Man.

Your wife won't feel loved, your kids won't feel safe, your friends won't seek you out for wisdom, and your relationship with God will be superficial and hollow. And in some part of your mind and heart, you'll know it.

You'll either be self-righteously religious or self-destructively rebellious. But you won't be a responsible, trustworthy man who is resting in the grace of Jesus.

It is the grace of Jesus Christ that reaches down to the lowest pit to find you and has the strength to pull you up and out. If you know anything about the reality of your own sin, that's no small feat. It's supernatural. God's arm is neither too short, nor too weak to save.

You can't climb out on your own. You can't jump out. You can't earn your way out or buy your way out. And you can't BS your way out. You can't balance the scales of cosmic justice with your good works. You can't hitch a ride on someone else's coattails. Your good deeds don't impress God if you're relying on them to save you. No false religion, or woke perversion of Christianity provides an ounce of help.

It is the grace of Jesus that pierces your heart of stone and powerfully transforms it into a heart of flesh. Grace alone has the power to crush a man's pride and forgive a man's sin. Grace has the ability to chase a man down who is running away. Grace saves. Rescues. Redeems. And rebuilds. That's no simple or easy task.

*"You then, my son, be **strong** in the **grace** that is in Christ Jesus."*

Paul, an Apostle of Jesus Christ, a spiritual father to Timothy, points Timothy to find his strength in the grace of Jesus. A man becomes truly strong when he receives and begins to understand and walk in the overwhelming grace of God.

It's not about who can burp the loudest, swim the farthest, lift the most, shoot the best, make the most money, score the most touchdowns, get with the most girls, drive the biggest truck, grow the best beard, sport the best tattoos, or win fantasy football. It's not about a man 'pulling himself up by his own bootstraps.'

A Stronger Man is a man who knows he needs, then requests and receives, the grace of God through Jesus Christ. A Stronger Man is a humble man—a man who looks to God, submits to God, follows Jesus, trusts Jesus, obeys Jesus, and stands his ground in the face of temptation.

Brothers, we get our strength from the grace of Jesus.

You need grace. You need more grace. You'll always need grace. You're not strong if you think you don't need it. You're weak, deceived, and in danger.

Clear so far?

So, what does grace have to do with our identity as sons? Stronger Men live as loved sons.

Not every man will become a father. But every man is a son.

We all had earthly dads, for better or for worse, but we also have access through the grace of Jesus Christ to our perfect, heavenly Father.

And God places us in the family of God, the Church, where we have access to spiritual fathers, mentors, teachers, examples, and a band of brothers.

The Apostle Paul begins his second letter to Timothy and addresses him as follows: *"To Timothy, my dear son: Grace, mercy and peace from God the Father and Christ Jesus our Lord."*

Again, at the beginning of chapter two, after calling Timothy to guard the deposit of the gospel and remain faithful to Jesus Christ in an increasingly hostile and antagonistic culture, as a spiritual father nearing the end of his life, he writes:

"You then, my son, be strong in the grace that is in Christ Jesus."

"My dear son." "My son."

How do you think those words landed on Timothy? How would they land on you?

Timothy didn't have a godly dad. He first learned about Jesus from his grandmother and his mother. Then God brought another godly man—a spiritual father—into his life, the Apostle Paul.

If you had an active, loving, present, godly father, what would be the impact of hearing him say those words?

If you didn't (or don't) have an active, loving, present, godly father, what do you think would be the impact of those words?

Years ago, as a young youth pastor and Bible college student, I had the opportunity over four summers to work with an organization that served abused and neglected children in the greater Seattle area. It was a Christian organization that partnered with social services and the foster care system. All of the children who attended the week-long summer camp and program had heartbreaking stories. The behavioral problems and emotional damage were evident.

These were kids, ages 9-14, who would be the first to get kicked out of any other "regular camp." They had suffered from all manner of abuse, had been in and out of many different homes, had witnessed unspeakable horror in their short lives, and most didn't even know, let alone have, any positive relationship with their dad—that seemed to be the most common factor.

My first year serving, I was a camp counselor. I completed hours of training, and the needs of the kids were so great we maintained a 1:2 ratio of counselors to campers, with additional support staff, including professional social workers.

I'll never forget my first two campers. I'll call them "Tommy" and "Jack." Tommy and his twin brother had witnessed their dad murder their mom, and their dad was now serving a life sentence in prison. Tommy was a survivor. Amazingly, he had a joy about him on the surface, and he loved the connection with the other campers and soaked up the attention. His brother was much more reserved and inward-focused. Tommy was doing his best to look after his brother.

In just seven days, Tommy trusted me and leaned into me for hugs and affirmation. On the last day of the camp, as the last Bible story session was ending, Tommy leaned over, hugged my side, looked up at me with his big brown eyes, and asked me, "Will you be my dad?" I was 21 years old. His words blew me away.

He was 11 years old at that time, and I wasn't allowed to have any contact with him outside that week of camp until he turned 18. He'd

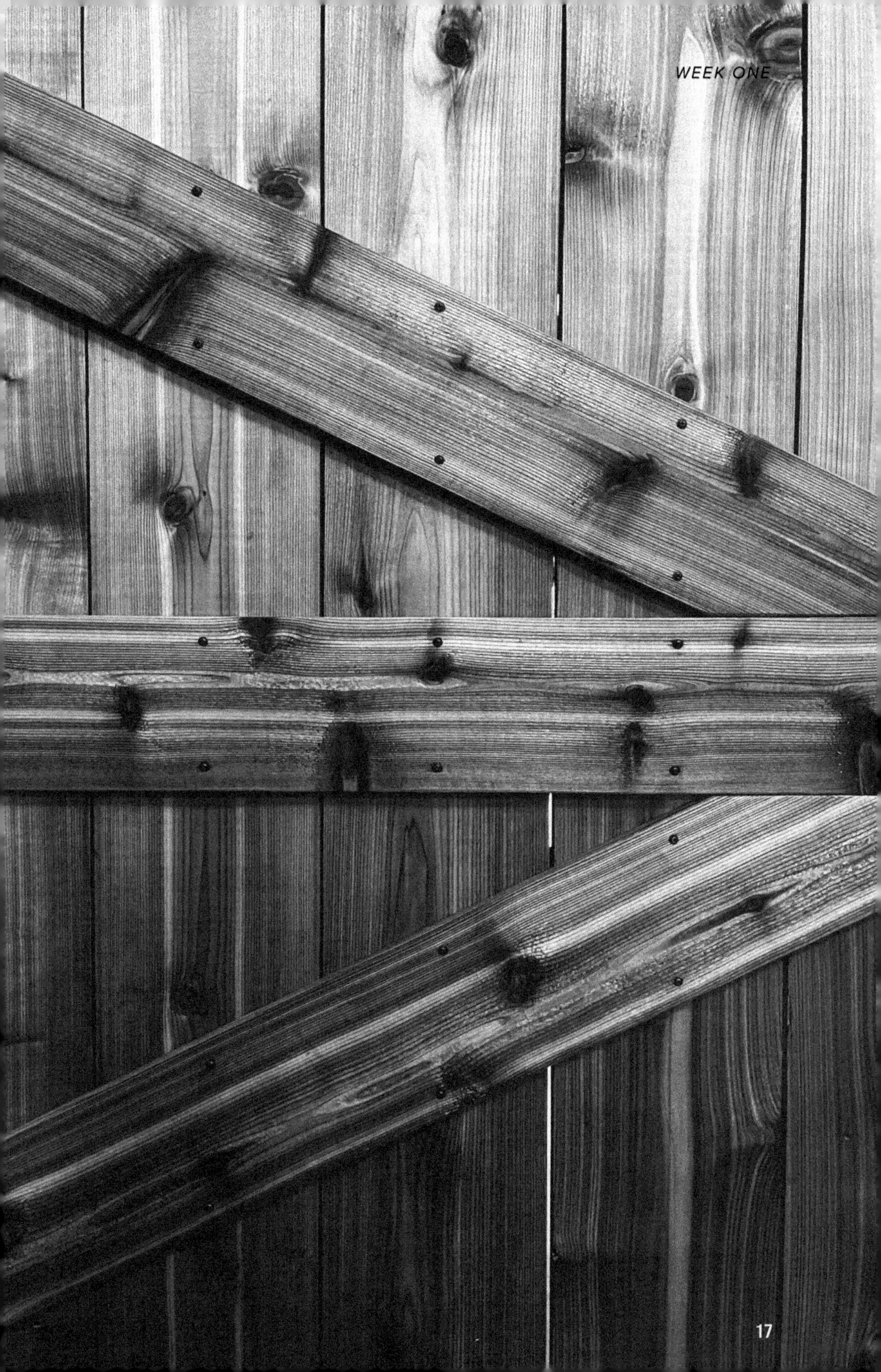

be 36 years old today. I have no idea where Tommy is today or if he's even still alive.

Jack was a year older. Still wetting the bed most nights. He had been in and out of more foster homes than the number of years he'd been alive. No stability. No security. No dad. Before the last day ended, Jack asked me, "Could I live with you?"

I still think about Tommy and Jack to this day, 25 years later.

I have names and faces and voices in my mind when I read in **Psalm 68:5**, "*God is a father to the fatherless.*"

I now have four children of my own. Two daughters and two sons.

They all have an earthly dad, and they all need their heavenly Father. "My dear son."

Those words carry power.

Dads are powerful. God made it that way. All fatherhood derives its name from God Himself (Ephesians 3:14). But sin entered the picture and brought a devastating curse. We have been separated from our Creator, alienated by our sin, and cut off from the source of our deepest identity.

I've now been in some form of vocational ministry for 25 years: 10 years as a youth pastor and 15 years in church planting and pastoring adults.

All too often, it's not easy or enjoyable for men to talk about their dads. The conversation can quickly get awkward, quiet, avoidant, or weighty. Sometimes, guys light up and love to talk about their dads. In my experience, they are, sadly, more of the minority.

So I know the territory I'm stepping into. I know the risk I'm taking in writing this, and perhaps, you're taking a risk in reading this. Stay with me.

I want to say up front, if your dad is a source of pain or anger for you, this book isn't about pointlessly digging up junk, nursing a never-ending wound, feeling sorry for yourself, or bashing your dad. There may be things you read that bug you, confuse you, bring up memories or painful emotions, or make you react. I'd simply ask that you hang in here with me and stay open to hear what the Bible has to say about the power of knowing God as your Father and the blessing, healing, and strength that comes from knowing Jesus as the Way, the Truth, and the Life, Who brings us into restored relationship with the Father.

No matter what kind of dad you had, or what kind of story you have, there is really, really good news for men in the pages and words of the Bible that I want to highlight for us as men.

Thankfully, stories like Tommy's and Jack's aren't the only kind. There are many dads who are in the fight, doing their best to raise their sons the best they know how with the examples, teaching, and tools they have. Including men reading this right now.

Thankfully, God is again stirring the hearts of men and fathers to become Stronger Men, who pass on a legacy of faithfulness and the blessing of a godly dad.

No matter where we started or where we are, it starts by becoming Stronger Men, through the grace of Jesus Christ, who are set free to love as loved sons.

LET'S PRAY

Father, thank You for the man, young or old, holding this book. Use these words and these pages, and above all, Your Word, as the truth that sets free, makes new, and gives strength to build us up and make us a blessing to those around us. Show us our need for grace and our access to it, to You, through Jesus. Prepare our hearts to receive what You have for us, and by Your grace, make us Stronger Men, as loved sons. In Jesus' Name, amen.

FROM A STRONGER MAN

When I sit down to reflect on my childhood I'm struck with a myriad of emotions. It's interesting to look back over the years and try to remember something that truly feels like another life. I feel as though I am attempting to watch family videos on an old 8mm projector and the screen is cracked and faded. What I do remember is fractured, distant, and far away. Even as I write tears pour down my face. Not because of the hardship I may have endured, but because of the grace I have received.

My story starts like many others, I was born into a normal household, with normal parents doing the best they could with what they had. Unfortunately, what they had was an inheritance of sin. My father was a diagnosed manic depressant. His depression sent him down the trail of drugs and alcohol and his outburst of manic put him in a rage where he would abuse my mom. I have one older brother. He had it harder than me because he was old enough to remember my dad. I am grateful to say I only know this because of the stories my mom would tell. She left my dad when I was 1-year-old and began the long, hard journey of raising two young boys as a single mother. Having three kids of my own, I could not imagine what it would be like to not only be the primary provider, but also the caretaker of the home. I honor my mother for this. She did the best she could with what she had. This sent her on a spiritual journey, and that journey led her to what is known as paganism. This became the religion of my household. I have memories of attending weekly séance's, festivals in the mountains, and everything you could imagine surrounding that kind of lifestyle. To say the least, I grew up fast.

My mother remarried when I was seven. There is not a lot to say about my step dad. He was not as physically abusive like my real dad, but he was a man consumed by anger. He tried to suppress that anger with drug use. My brother found my step dad's stash of marijuana and I remember smoking weed for the first time while waiting for the bus when I was eight. This started my own addiction with drugs that lasted almost 20 years. We moved every year of my life. I ended up going to 13 different schools, around 20 different homes, over 5 states. After my freshman year of high school, it was time to move again. Using divination and witchcraft, my mom picked a little town off a map, 1,200 miles to the north of where we were living in Colorado, called Wenatchee. I finished up high school, graduated when I was 16, and immediately moved out of the house. I began my slow decline into full on madness. Drinking every night, smoking all day, everyday, doing whatever I wanted, whenever I wanted. This lasted for almost 10 years and then something incredible happened. God intervened.

My girlfriend at the time invited me to a small church called Grace Covenant Church. This would be the first time I had attended a church in my life. I'll admit, I was only going to keep my girlfriend happy, which didn't work out because she broke up with me shortly after I started to attend. I remember being at a crossroads—I could stop going to church altogether, or I could lean in and give this Christian thing a real try. I chose to lean in and God began to draw me to Him. He gave me the one thing I never had. A father. Through the men of Grace City, He revealed Himself as my true heavenly Father.

I was a fully forgiven, adopted son. Fast forward over 10 years...I am a father myself. I married the most beautiful, godly, astonishing woman: the love of my life, Bonnie. We have three kids and God has given me the holy opportunity to work as close as I can with Jesus and the Holy Spirit to finally break the curse of sin that I inherited from my father. When God says He can make you new, it's not just a spiritual reality happening behind some hidden veil, but a physical reality that changes you to the very core of who you are. God has granted me a new life. I am free. I am changed. I am a son of God.

Chaz, 37

REFLECT & DISCUSS

1. What is your biggest takeaway from this chapter? What caught your attention as you read it?

_____

_____

_____

2. What comes to mind when you think of the word "grace?" Is it a strong word or weak word? How does this affect your concept of what it means to be a Stronger Man?

_____

_____

_____

3. Why is it crucial to understand the relationship between "grace" and "strength" in relationship to true manhood?

_____

_____

_____

4. How would you describe your relationship with your earthly father? What were/are his strengths? What were/are his weaknesses?

_____

_____

_____

5. Are there other men God has brought into your life who impacted you positively, like a spiritual father or an Apostle Paul? What attributes and qualities did/do they possess?

_____

_____

_____

6. What does it mean to "live like a loved son?" Has there been a defining moment or season in your life when you realized and experienced the love of God for you?

_____

_____

_____

7. What do you hope to gain from this book? In what ways do you want to grow as a stronger, godly man?

_____

_____

_____

TAKE ACTION

- Connect with other men using this study. If you're not currently meeting with a small group of men to read, discuss, and encourage one another, make a list of some men you know who you could reach out to and see if there is interest to connect and meet and discuss the book together. If you have a group of men, text them with a follow-up thought or encouragement from this chapter before your next meeting.

- If you have a son, let him know you are reading this book and share one thing that has encouraged you or challenged you already.

- If possible, let your dad know you are reading this book and share one thing that has encouraged you or challenged you already.

WEEK 2

REVIVE THE MEN,
REVERSE THE CURSE

Behold, I will send you Elijah the prophet before the great and awesome day of the Lord comes. **AND HE WILL TURN THE HEARTS OF FATHERS TO THEIR CHILDREN AND THE HEARTS OF CHILDREN TO THEIR FATHERS,** lest I come and strike the land with a curse.

MALACHI 4:5-6

As the men go, so goes the family.

As the family goes, so goes the Church.

As the Church goes, so goes the culture.

When men fail to love and lead their families, a curse of destruction always follows.

We see the evidence of this curse all through our society. Fatherless homes and rebellious sons litter our streets and fill our prisons, universities, boardrooms, stadiums, and bars.

Men are checked out. Many haven't even left their mom's basement. Too many are unwilling to work as they look for safe spaces to contemplate the microaggressions that leave them questioning their gender. They paint their nails and parade in dresses. They wave the rainbow flag and label any sign of masculine strength as toxic. They want you to pay off their student loans and legalize their sexually perverse fetish.

Society is literally teetering on the precipice of collapse. The most basic truths are rejected. The most evil and perverse acts are celebrated and defended.

We are witnessing the judgment of God. Our culture is at flood-like levels of debauchery and, rather than flooding the earth like He did in the days of Noah and promised never to do again, God is giving people over to their perverse and sinful desires. His hand of blessing and protection has lifted. And the curse of judgment is picking up steam.

How do we reverse the curse?

Where are the men of God?

When God sets out to restore and rebuild His people and bless a nation, He starts with the men.

That's what Malachi 4 tells us. He turns the hearts of fathers to their children and the hearts of children to their fathers. This "turning" is what the Bible calls repentance. And when that happens in the hearts of men, revival is underway.

Wake up the men! Wake up the fathers! Restore the family! Return to the Lord!

The prophet Malachi wrote the last book of the Old Testament. He wrote at a time when the culture was godless. The people of God—

including their leaders—were weak and compromised. Their priorities were wrong, their hearts astray. Even though God is a loving Father, and a great King over His people, their hearts were far from Him and they were not honoring the Lord. Divorce was rampant, the family broken, greed and covetousness filled their hearts, they "played church," robbed God by withholding tithes, and made a mockery of true worship.

Like Cain in Genesis, they didn't bring their best offerings from a sincere heart of worship followed by a life of faith-filled loving obedience.

God always raised up prophets to warn of judgment to come on the wicked and unrepentant, and to also comfort the humble with promises of hopeful restoration and blessing for those who would repent. And Malachi was no different.

There are at least two realities that jump off the page to me in the last nine verses of Malachi. These seem to be preconditions to the reviving, restoring work of God in any generation. The curse can be reversed, at least in part, until the ultimate reversal at the second coming of Jesus.

Listen to **Malachi 3:16-18**,

Then those who feared the Lord spoke with one another. The Lord paid attention and heard them, and a book of remembrance was written before Him of those who feared the Lord and revered His name. "They shall be mine," says the Lord of hosts, "in the day when I make up my treasured possession, and I will spare them as a man spares his son who serves him. Then once more you shall see the distinction between the righteous and the wicked, between one who serves God and one who does not serve Him."'

And **Malachi 4:1-6** continues,

"For behold, the day is coming, burning like an oven, when all the arrogant and all evildoers will be stubble. The day that is coming shall set them ablaze, says the Lord of hosts, so that it will leave them neither root nor branch. But for you who fear (revere) my name, the sun of righteousness shall rise with healing in its wings. You shall go out leaping like calves from the stall. And you shall tread down the wicked, for they will be ashes under the soles of your feet, on the day when I act, says the Lord of hosts."

"Remember the law of my servant Moses, the statutes and rules that I commanded him at Horeb for all Israel."

"Behold, I will send you Elijah the prophet before the great and awesome day of the Lord comes. And he will turn the hearts of fathers to their children and the hearts of children to their fathers, lest I come and strike the land with a decree of utter destruction."

Where does revival and restoration start? How will we once again see a distinction between the righteous and the wicked? How can we avoid or reverse a devastating curse on the land?

Revere His Name + Revive His Men = Reverse the Curse

It starts with the fear of the Lord and the It starts with the fear of the Lord and the work of repentance in the hearts of men, or, more specifically, fathers.

Revival is preceded and followed by the reconciliation and restoration of the family—of fathers and sons, sons and fathers—through men repenting out of a healthy and renewed fear and reverence for the Lord.

These were the last prophetic words of God recorded in the Old Testament before 400 years of silence.

The New Testament opens with John the Baptist appearing on the scene, coming in the spirit and power of Elijah, preaching a message of repentance, and preparing the way of the Lord, the Messiah—Jesus Christ—who came to usher in a new day of spiritual life and blessing and restoration, giving a foretaste of the freedom and healing of the Kingdom of God and the great day of the Lord.

Jesus came preaching the good news of the Kingdom of God and announced liberty for captives and sight for the blind. The lame began to walk and could once again leap like calves released from the stall as they proclaimed the praises of a merciful God who had not abandoned them to the curse forever.

The spirit of Elijah is still alive through the message of repentance from Stronger Men who are not afraid to preach truth in the face of a perverted culture and a compromised Church. The freedom of Jesus is still available through the power of the Holy Spirit to all those who repent.

Redemption and healing are available. Restoration and freedom are within reach. These are still the days of salvation. These are still the days of repentance. The Lord is not slow in returning or slow to keep His promises but is being patient to allow for men to wake up and return to the Lord, raise their sons, and bless their families and society around them by living truthfully in the face of lies.

We need to, once again, see sin as sin. Evil as evil. Lies as lies. Wickedness as wickedness.

It's time to fear the Lord.

The Bible says in **Proverbs 9:10**, "*The fear of the Lord is the beginning of wisdom.*"

The fear of the Lord brings light to the eyes and life to the bones. It's not a fear that causes one to run and hide but a fear that causes one to bow and draw near in humble repentance and brokenness.

Psalm 25:14 says, "*The Lord confides in those who fear Him, He makes His covenant known to them.*" Intimacy, nearness, and friendship with the Lord are reserved for those who fear Him.

Where are the men who can weep over their sin?

Where are the men who don't see themselves as victims of others' actions but recognize their own sin and rebellion and responsibility for their own choices?

Where are the men who are ready to stop blame-shifting, minimizing, justifying, excusing, or denying their responsibility?

Where are the men who love the Lord with all their heart, mind, soul and strength?

Where are the men who long to see Jesus glorified and lifted high and live for the glory of God and for the fame and renown of His Name alone?

Where are the men who revere the Lord and reject all manner of sin and compromise? Whose greatest passions are not the trivial things that selfish men chase incessantly?

Brothers, let us be done with lesser things. Let us abandon trivial pursuits. Let us sacrifice selfish idols and aimless ambitions.

What if you went all in on living for Jesus?

What if what you feared the most wasn't what others thought of you or the threat of losing your job or the securing of boyhood dreams or the accumulation of toys or a massive retirement portfolio?

What if, instead, you were possessed with a longing and a passion to be a part of a once-in-a-generation, once-in-a-lifetime move of God where men return to the Lord in droves? Where families thrive in healthy churches. Where boys become Stronger Men and girls become noble women.

What if there stirred, for the first time in your chest, a consuming hunger for the Word of God? What if you saw, with fresh eyes, God as your Father turning toward you? And you, in turn, turned toward Him?

What if God's sons turned toward God? Where are those men?

I believe one of them is holding this book in his hands, right now, reading this very sentence.

Welcome to the few. Welcome to a remnant of those who revere His Name.

Your Father in Heaven loves you and wants you to daily turn toward Him as you live in the freedom of repentance and the joy of the fear of the Lord, with the healing rays of the Son of righteousness on your face, as you live out your days as a Stronger Man, bringing blessing—reversing the curse—wherever you go.

LET'S PRAY

Father, break our hearts with the open mockery of Your Name. Restore to us, as men, a deep reverence for Your glory and honor, first in our own hearts and lives, and also in our sons and daughters, and in the people of God. Teach us what it means to fear the Lord and to walk in the glorious liberty and freedom of righteousness, healing, and the joy that comes through repentance. Use us to raise up a generation who knows and serves the Lord. Revive my heart today, in Jesus' Name, amen.

FROM A STRONGER MAN

When I was young my father left. I was around five or six when he left. I don't have many memories from that young stage of my life, but I still remember that night. With razor sharp focus, I remember running through the dark, out in the farm yard chasing the tail lights down the driveway. Calling as loud as I could "Dad come back!" He never touched the brakes. He just drove away, out of my life forever. That night my dad didn't just leave me, he left our family, he walked away from his ministry as a pastor, and away from God.

I spent the next 30 years of my life chasing everything that the world said would fill the void in my soul. I threw everything I could at the crater-sized hole in my heart, yet it was never enough. It wasn't easy growing up without a father, though I fully acknowledge that I had it far better than some. Still, having to fake your way through life because there was no dad to teach you how to drive a nail, throw a spiral, shoot a rifle, or swing an ax, isn't the best way to grow up. There was no YouTube when I grew up. The only way you learned how to be a man was from another man.

So I turned to the world to teach and arm me how to be what the world says a "man" is. Sure I got tough...in some ways, but oh so weak in others. I used to bare knuckle box for fun, chew cope without spitting, and shoot whiskey like water. But on the inside, I was broken and afraid. Terrified that I would be exposed for what I was. I was a scared kid who never had a dad to tell him he was good enough.

During those 30 years, I spent a lot of time doing all the wrong things. Terrible things I deeply regret. Then about two years ago, I came to a Christmas Eve Eve service at Grace City Church. I came just to satisfy my mother's wishes, but what happened that night was nothing short of a miracle. God grabbed a hold of my heart and touched a place in my soul that was buried so far down that I didn't even know it existed anymore. Something changed that night in my life. Over the next several days, weeks, and months things started to happen to me. I was remade. It wasn't easy, but God put my heart in the forge—He went down deep into the places of my soul that only He could access. On the anvil and through the fire, He reshaped me and purified me.

During that time, things were happening in my life that I could not explain. I remember walking through a hayfield one evening after work, talking out loud to God. I was bitterly complaining about my father—how he left me, how he broke our family. Blaming him for all the wretched things that I had done in my life. In mid-sentence, God cut me off and spoke to me. He said, "Who are you? Who are you to condemn that man? Have you forgotten the things you have done? The things I have forgiven you of? You are no better than that man."

In that moment, God reminded me of all the horrible things I had done and the choices I had made in my own life. My own wretchedness. And He reminded me of the love and grace that He poured out upon me. The forgiveness He gave that I did nothing to deserve. And in the very same moment, God allowed me to feel the pain that my father had carried the past 30 years, the guilt, the shame, and the sorrow for the choice that he made. I felt the heartache of my father who missed out on his family for 30 years. No birthdays, no sports, no memories at all. I suddenly knew that I was no better than him and in some ways had done far worse.

The LORD continued to speak to me and I knew I had to find my father. I had to look him in the eyes and tell him I love him, that I forgive him, and that I was sorry for not being a good son. I should have forgiven my father long ago. The LORD told me to take my father's Bible back to him that my mother had faithfully kept all those years. God told me it was time that book went back to him. And God told me to show my father his own name written down on the front corner of that old bible and to tell my dad that God still knows him by name. That He knows the hairs on his head and that He will never leave nor forsake him. That it was time my dad quit running away—time to turn around and face the LORD.

So that's exactly what I did. I got on a train and found my dad. I was able to do everything that the LORD told me to do. Today, my father and I have one of the sweetest relationships I could ask for. We regularly talk on the phone and I see him often. Our conversations are always centered on Jesus and we talk about the goodness and faithfulness of God. My father was at my wedding this past year and he echoed the LORD's words to me: "You are my son, of whom I am well pleased." Those 10 words from God, then from my dad, did more for my soul than 30 years of anything this world could ever promise.

Jake, 37

REFLECT & DISCUSS &

1. What is your biggest takeaway from this chapter? What stood out to you as you read?

_____

_____

_____

2. How would you describe the times we are living in? In particular, how would you describe the "state of boys/men" today? What are the biggest lies that our society is telling and believing about men?

_____

_____

_____

3. What does it look like for a man to "revere the Lord?" What does "reverence" involve?

_____

_____

_____

4. How would you describe the "distinction" that needs to be restored between righteousness and wickedness? What are some of the core differences between a man who serves the Lord and a man who doesn't?

_____

_____

_____

5. What goes into "reviving men?" What does that involve? What are ways you see men being reached and revived effectively today?

_____

_____

_____

6. Why do you think the father-son relationship is so powerful and important?

_____

_____

_____

7. Do you have any examples of ways you have seen "the curse reversed" in a family or situation as a result of deep repentance and change in a man's life?

_____

_____

_____

_____

TAKE ACTION

- Write out a prayer of repentance that expresses your desire to be a Stronger Man. Where do you need to grow and change in your relationship with the Lord? What gets in the way? What distractions and temptations do you encounter on a daily or weekly basis? Confess this honestly to the Lord.

- If you don't have a home church, find a faithful, Bible-teaching church in your area and commit to gathering regularly. If you have a home church, what's your next step of growth in your relationship and commitment there? Take that step this week.

WEEK 3

REDEEMED FROM THE EMPTY WAY OF LIFE

For you know that it was not with perishable things such as silver or gold that YOU WERE REDEEMED FROM THE EMPTY WAY OF LIFE HANDED DOWN TO YOU FROM YOUR FOREFATHERS, but with the precious blood of Christ, a lamb without blemish or defect.

1 PETER 1:17-19

This book is all about good news. One of the things that makes good news "good" is that it gives you hope.

Humans need hope to live. When a person loses hope, they stop truly living.

Christianity is largely about hope. Not mere wishful thinking like, "I hope it doesn't rain tomorrow." But true hope. A confident expectation of fulfillment and a positive future.

Peter opens his first letter with these words in verses 3-5:

> *Praise be to the God and Father of our Lord Jesus Christ! In His great mercy He has given us new birth into a living hope through the resurrection of Jesus Christ from the dead, and into an inheritance that can never perish, spoil or fade. This inheritance is kept in Heaven for you, who through faith are shielded by God's power until the coming of the salvation that is ready to be revealed in the last time.*

The gospel doesn't just give you hope, it gives you "a living hope."

A hope that can endure through trial and pain and suffering and failure. Peter himself knew the power of having his hope restored. He once hung his head in defeat, thinking he was destined to failure. But Jesus renewed his hope. Three times Jesus spoke words of affirmation and life-giving hope to Peter in the aftermath of Peter's denial of Christ.

Without hope, men won't rise to the high call of Stronger Manhood and glorious sonship.

Many men hang their head in failure, guilt, shame, fear, and defeat. The enemy uses these weapons relentlessly against men.

He loves to take our past or our pedigree— or lack thereof—and convince us we're disqualified or destined for failure.

He tries to equate the failures of our dads or our grandpas with our identity or destiny. "You're a joke. Just like your dad. And his dad. That's all you'll ever be!"

That, my friends, is a lie!

Enter the Good News and power of the Cross of Jesus.

Your past doesn't have to define you. In Christ, it doesn't.

Your dad's failures and shortcomings don't have to be yours. In Christ, they aren't.

If there's generational baggage and filth in your lineage, you don't have to pack it around any longer, and you don't have to hand it off to your children either. In Christ, you can become a new link in a new chain.

All the baggage, sin, failure, and garbage can be defeated and transformed by the power of Jesus.

You can be redeemed from the empty way of life handed down to you from your forefathers.

It's one of the most powerful and beautiful promises in the Bible.

In fact, in Christ, you're either a steward or a starter. If you've been given a godly legacy, you can steward it. If you haven't, you can start it.

And by God's grace, you can avoid being a stumbling block to future generations.

Peter continues in chapter 1:13-21:

> *Therefore, with minds that are alert and fully sober, set your hope on the grace to be brought to you when Jesus Christ is revealed at His coming. As obedient children, do not conform to the evil desires you had when you lived in ignorance. But just as He who called you is holy, so be holy in all you do; for it is written: "Be holy, because I am holy." Since you call on a Father who judges each person's work impartially, live out your time as foreigners here in reverent fear. For you know that it was not with perishable things such as*

silver or gold that you were redeemed from the empty way of life handed down to you from your forefathers, but with the precious blood of Christ, a lamb without blemish or defect. He was chosen before the creation of the world, but was revealed in these last times for your sake. Through Him you believe in God, who raised Him from the dead and glorified Him, and so your faith and hope are in God.

Notice again the prominence and repetition of "hope."

Hear the call to live as obedient children, calling on your new heavenly Father.

Your former "old" evil desires no longer have the last word.

Now, you're called to holiness. And now, in Christ, we are careful in how we live, recognizing that we are foreigners in this world. We don't treat our new life lightly; we don't short sell the grace of God and the change Jesus has made in our lives. Why? Because it wasn't with perishable things like silver or gold that we have been redeemed but with the precious blood of Christ.

We've been bought with a price! We've been ransomed! Redeemed!

And what is it that we've been redeemed from? Notice what Peter says. In Christ, you have been *"redeemed from the empty way of life handed down to you from your forefathers."*

What does that mean? It means the chains of generational sin, bondage, and baggage have been broken in Christ.

Stop and think for a moment. What comes to mind as you think about what was handed down to you from your dad or granddad, and what you might hand down to your children and grandchildren?

Whatever hopeless thought you've been tempted to believe before, you can now fight with the truth and promise of 1 Peter 1:18.

Your broken family history does not have to become your future legacy. In Christ, you get a new family tree and you can start a new family line.

You're free to be faithful where your forefathers failed. You're not defined by your dad's addictions.

You're not limited by your family drama.

Addiction, abandonment, adultery, anger, abuse, arrogance, apathy. None of it has to follow you into your future! In Jesus' Name!

Suicide, divorce, depression, pornography, lying, cowardice. Nailed to the cross! Powerless over your life!

The emptiness that was handed down to you was hung on the cross and therefore doesn't have to hang around your neck.

What would it look like for you to walk in newness of life without disqualifying yourself or excusing yourself because of some lie of the enemy tied to some generational sin or failure of your dad? Or your dad's dad? Or your dad's dad's dad?

What if you were now free to start a new line of generational blessing and godliness?

It's not mere wishful thinking or too good to be true. It's the living hope that you're given through faith in Jesus Christ. Your past, present, and future can be redeemed by the blood of Jesus.

Your new family tree is the Cross of Jesus Christ, the tree of Calvary.

Stronger men live like redeemed sons who leave behind the empty ways of life handed down to them from their forefathers.

As lovers of a great and gracious Savior, with a new Father to live for, Stronger Men leave a new and better legacy

LET'S PRAY

Father, thank You for sending Jesus to redeem our lives from the pit and to free us to steward or start a legacy of generational faithfulness. I pray for the man reading this who battles fear or lies because of his broken past or broken family. Show him the power of his new family tree in Christ, the Cross of Jesus. Grant him confident hope to start a new line of faith. And I pray for the man reading this who is endeavoring to steward the blessing of a godly dad. Fill him with confident hope and deep gratitude as he adds more logs to the generational fire of faithfulness. May it burn hotter and brighter than ever to the glory of Jesus.

FROM A STRONGER MAN

My dad did the best he knew how...or, at least, that's what I prefer to believe. He was the product of a different generation than today. Some of it better, some of it worse. One of six kids in a long line of farmers, the boys, especially, were taught to be tough and worked on the farm at an early age. My dad worked 16-hour days from spring to fall, at the expense of school, friends, hobbies, and sleep. Back then, you could get a hug from your mom and scripture from church, but you didn't expect any attention from your dad unless you screwed up.

As a teenager, my dad left the farm for college, married my mom, and I was their firstborn. He had no training or good examples to draw from. Despite this, he was a good provider and a moral, conservative man that took us to church and the great outdoors. On the downside, he was an arrogant, impatient perfectionist that sabotaged any hope for close relationships with his kids.

In the early years I was a normal, happy, middle-class kid. My life was full of friends, camping, boating, church, road trips, little league baseball, Boy Scouts, and lots of Christmas presents.

Life was good until the age of 12. We moved across town and everything changed. At this very impressionable age, our short, 3-mile relocation meant a new school for me, and the loss of all my classmates and teachers. With only three months left at the elementary school I grew up in, I went from being the fun-loving, popular, class clown with good grades, to a lonely "new kid" trying to make friends in a strange place. I started skipping school to avoid my new awkward reality. The lack of good friends or mentors opened the door for bad relationships to form, and that eventually led to total rebellion against all forms of authority.

By the 7th grade, I was skipping school on a regular basis. I started drinking, smoking, vandalizing property, starting fights, and shoplifting. I was fooling around with girls when I was 15. As soon as I could drive, I was earning tickets for speeding and reckless driving.

When I was 16, I dropped out of high school. I went back when I was 17 but dropped out again. That was the same year, I got my girlfriend pregnant and her parents convinced her to have an abortion. We were married by the age of 20 but divorced six months later when she found someone at college that treated her better. No shocker there.

I sank into a deep depression just in time for my 21st birthday, so now my poor choices could be on full display at the bars. It wasn't hard to find desperate women in these locales, so I fooled myself into thinking I was a pretty big deal.

Not surprisingly, I was caught drinking and driving twice around this time. After spending a few hours inside a small concrete room with a stainless steel toilet, I started imagining what life would be like if this was my permanent residence. I knew I needed to change but old habits die hard.

By the age of 22, I was a divorced, womanizing, alcoholic, suicidal, high school dropout, with two DUI's and a part-time job at a bowling alley. I had no hope and I was completely lost.

Then my mom encouraged me to visit a new church she heard about. I wasn't very interested in the church part, but when I heard they had a young adults group, I surmised the prospects for a long term relationship were better at church on Sunday morning than the tavern on Saturday night.

I wasn't ready for what happened next. Every Sunday, I heard the gospel preached and I met the nicest people. After a couple months of the pastor reading my mail, I was convicted by the Holy Spirit and gave my life to Jesus.

I confessed that I was a sinner and I repented. In that moment, my heavenly Father forgave my sins and adopted me into His family. He gave me purpose to live for and hope for the future.

I am still shocked, to this day, by the reality of Jesus' perfect life and substitutionary atoning death to reconcile me to a Holy God so I could spend eternity with Him.

When God saved me, He broke the generational patterns that came before me and started a new family tree. I've been married to my amazing wife now for 25 years and have two grown daughters that love me and follow Jesus! I'm not a perfect father, but when it comes to my kids, I've always been very intentional with my time, attention, affection, and encouragement. Most importantly, I remind them of their identity in Christ, and direct their attention to our heavenly Father who is perfect and loves them even more than I do.

I'm eternally grateful to Jesus for saving me, my wife, and my daughters. All praise and glory and honor to my Lord and Savior, Jesus Christ!

Evan, 49

REFLECT & DISCUSS

1. What is your biggest takeaway from this chapter? What stood out to you as you read?

_____

_____

_____

2. How would you describe the "empty ways" that were handed down to you? What sin patterns or struggles can you identify that may run in your family?

_____

_____

_____

3. How does this passage in 1 Peter give you hope or encouragement? What does it teach you about the difference following Jesus makes?

_____

_____

_____

4. On a scale of 1-10, how would you describe your current level of "hope" in your life and relationships? What is pulling it down? What could pull it up?

_____

_____

_____

5. What are some of the lies and accusations the enemy tries to whisper in your mind about your past or your future? How can you combat these thoughts with the gospel truth the next time these come?

_____

_____

_____

6. What are some of the lies and accusations the enemy tries to whisper in your mind about your past or your future? How can you combat these thoughts with the gospel truth the next time these come?

_____

_____

_____

7. Who are some other men in your life who you could encourage with this passage in 1 Peter this week? Write down their names. Pray for them. Look for an open door opportunity to encourage them in person or with a text or phone call.

_____

_____

_____

TAKE ACTION

- Write a rough draft note or letter to your dad. At this point, don't worry about whether you give it to him or not. Just write out the thoughts that come. This is for you. What do you want/need to say? What are you thankful for? What has been hard or painful? Pay attention to the thoughts and feelings that arise as you write.

- If you have a son, send a text of encouragement. Ask how you can pray for him this week.

- If possible, send a text of encouragement to your dad. Ask him how you can pray for him this week. If there is another significant father-figure in your life, send him a similar text.

WEEK 4

WELCOMING HOME THE LOST SON

So he got up and went to his father. But while he was still a long way off, his father saw him and was filled with compassion for him; he ran to his son, threw his arms around him and kissed him. The son said to him, 'Father, I have sinned against heaven and against you. I am no longer worthy to be called your son.' But the father said to his servants, 'Quick! Bring the best robe and put it on him. Put a ring on his finger and sandals on his feet. Bring the fattened calf and kill it. Let's have a feast and celebrate. **FOR THIS SON OF MINE WAS DEAD AND IS ALIVE AGAIN; HE WAS LOST AND IS FOUND.'** So they began to celebrate.

LUKE 15:20-24

This is arguably one of the greatest passages in the entire Bible. The parable of the lost son—the prodigal son.

Once you see the picture Jesus paints with His words in Luke 15, you will never think of or see God the same again in your life. This story reveals the heart of God, the heart of Christianity, and the heart of the Bible—as much as any text in the entire Bible.

The story begins with a father who has two sons. The younger brother is known as the rebellious prodigal, who spurns his dad's house and rules, demands his cut of the inheritance, and runs off in wild living. When the party ends and he's blown through his resources, he finds himself eating at the pig trough. He eventually comes to his senses, as he remembers the plenty of his father's house. He returns home ready to grovel in servitude only to encounter a shocking display of grace at the embrace of his father as he is graciously reinstated to the family with a lavish celebration.

The older brother is revealed as the religious rule-keeper who resents the grace his father shows to his brother and refuses to enter the welcome home party because he never left and he kept the rules and yet never got a party. His focus is on his remaining inheritance, which is funding the fattened calf and threatened by the restoration of the younger brother back into the family.

The spotlight of the story is largely on the father, whose heart is for both of his sons. He welcomes home the repentant younger son, as he watched daily for his return and as he ran down the road to embrace him. It's one of the most moving images in the world that strikes deeply at our hearts. Can you imagine your father running to welcome you home?

But the father also leaves the party to appeal to the offended older son, inviting him to repentance as this brother is now the one who is fracturing the family and needs to be restored.

It's a parable that displays the power of grace and the dangers of both rebellion and religion. It's the third story in a series of parables in Luke 15 all highlighting the importance of urgently searching for that which is lost: the lost sheep (15:3-7), the lost coin (15:8-10), and the lost son (15:11-32).

One of the key differences between the parable of the lost son and the stories about the sheep and the coin, is that there is no urgent search party sent out looking for that which is lost. In the first two parables, there's an urgent search party underway. But in the story of the son, no one goes out searching. That's weird. The father was looking and watching daily, waiting to see if his son was returning home. But the older brother stayed home. Maybe he should have been the one to lead the search party?

Which leads to another key difference between the parable of the lost son and the first two stories: the response when that which is lost is found.

In the first two, there is widespread rejoicing. And Jesus drives home the point that in the same way there is rejoicing in Heaven when one sinner repents. In the third story, the father rejoices and the party is thrown. The response of the older brother, however, stands in stark contrast to the other stories. He gets angry and offended and refuses to even join in the celebration!

Jesus told this parable in a crowd of pharisees who were upset that Jesus was eating with tax collectors and sinners. Jesus was welcoming tax collectors and sinners—younger brothers—and the Pharisees were acting like the offended older brother. Jesus is, in essence, exposing the dramatic distinction between the heart of the father and the heart of the self-righteous older brother, who was refusing to welcome and celebrate repentant sinners.

The punch line of the contrast is that Jesus Christ is revealing Himself to be the true and better older brother—the true and better Israel. Jesus Christ is the older brother who seeks and saves that which is lost. He's the older brother who gladly gives of His rightful inheritance and, at great cost to Himself, welcomes the younger brother home with extravagant grace. He's the older brother who celebrates with the Father the return of lost sons.

It's a moving story and powerful picture of the gospel.

Jesus Christ came to seek and to save the lost and bring us home to the Father. And the Father runs down the road to welcome us home.

Welcome home! For those who have come home to the Father through the Son, you're not a mere servant, and you could never work enough to earn your spot back in the family. You're a son who was dead and is now alive.

Here are 7 Truths Men Need To Understand and Embrace:

1 THE NATURE OF OUR SIN

Every one of us is a sinner by nature and choice. At the heart of our sin is the shaking of our fist at God, the rejection of His authority in our life, and our desire to live life on our own terms. Both sons ran away, just in different ways at different times. The younger brother revealed his heart against the father early, by overtly rebelling. He wanted to be in charge NOW. The older brother revealed his heart against the father later, but he revealed that he too had inwardly and covertly left long ago. He just figured he could be in charge later. Both forms of rebellion are deadly. Rejecting God's authority in your life, spurning His commands, rules, law, grace, and mercy leads to spiritual death. We're all rebellious. Some of us rebel by breaking the rules and leaving God and the Church. Others of us rebel by keeping the rules, pulling ourselves up by our bootstraps, thinking we're better than others, and thinking in our hearts that we know better how to run this place. In both cases, it's deadly sin that separates you from the Father and leaves you outside. While you may default one way or the other, the blunt reality is we all have both brothers in our hearts.

2 THE NEED FOR REPENTANCE

We all need to come to our senses. We all need to return home to the Father. This is the heart of repentance. The Greek word for repentance is "metanoia." It means "to change your mind." Or said another way, "to come to your senses." Repentance starts when we begin to think differently about God, about ourselves, about sin about what's right and wrong, and about which direction we need , to go. As this change of mind takes place, through the convicting and illuminating work of the Holy Spirit, we turn away from our sin and we turn to the Lord in repentance. While there is an important first time, this work of repentance in the Christian life is never a one- time reality. The first of Martin Luther's "95 Theses" that ignited the Protestant Reformation says, "When our Lord and Master Jesus Christ said 'Repent,' he intended that the entire life of believers should be repentance." Repentance is the initial and ongoing changing of our mind toward sin and toward the Lord that results in new action, new fruit, and new life. We never graduate beyond our need for repentance. We must continue to cultivate a heart of repentance.

3 THE HEART OF THE FATHER

Put yourself in the younger brother's shoes. What's he expecting on his long walk home? What will his dad say? How will he be received? He was prepared for the worst. His defenses were down. He was ready to confess and own up to the foolishness of his sin. He felt unworthy to be called his son. How did the father respond? This is what Jesus came to reveal—the heart of the Father. He ran to his broken son, wrapped his arms around him, kissed him, put on the robe, put on the ring, and killed the fattened calf. He welcomed his wayward son. This is how the Father responds to our repentance and return. Years ago, I had the opportunity to travel to St. Petersburg, Russia. During our time, we visited the Hermitage Museum where Rembrandt's famous painting of *The Prodigal Son* is on display. I stood in front of it, spellbound by the portrayal of the Father heart of God. Unless this lands deeply on a man, he won't know the joy of freedom or depth of grace. I am that son. You are that son. Foolish, sinful, broken, lost, dead. The Father welcomes me home, throws His arms around me, showers me with affection, affirmation, and assurance as His beloved son. If you've never been moved to tears by the love of the Father, there'll be a deficiency in your development as a lover of God and others.

4 THE NATURE OF GRACE

Grace in this story is lavish, extravagant, and costly. It offends both the rebellious and the religious. Any notion of pride or pity is confronted in its tracks by the grace of God. The younger son had his groveling speech prepared; he was ready to wallow in self-pity and feelings of unworth. He thought he would work as a slave and servant to somehow pay the father back or earn his place back in the family. No deal. Not a chance. Grace offends your self-pity and your poor-me posture. It demands that you lift your chin, receive the robe and ring, and come back to the family on God's terms only—by sheer grace. You're a son, not a slave. You must humbly receive it. Lots of men struggle with pity and false humility. Brother, let's slay that dragon.

Likewise, grace offends the older brother's pride who thinks he's earned the right to future blessing through his hard work and "clean" record. This makes him feel superior to others and resent grace and the generous cost of forgiveness. The Bible is clear, "*God opposes the proud but gives grace to the humble*." Pride kills, in both self-pity and self-righteous forms. Stronger Men slay this double-headed dragon with the sword of grace. Jesus was willing to absorb the cost of your forgiveness: He who was rich became poor so that in Him you might become rich (2 Corinthians 8:9). That's grace. Only the humble know they need it, and only the humble can actually receive it.

5 THE DANGER OF SELF-RIGHTEOUS RELIGION

There are two brothers who represent different ways of rejecting Jesus, but only one remains on the outside looking in at the end of the story. Jesus was putting the squeeze on the religious heart of the Pharisees. Self-righteous religion is doubly dangerous and deadly. And here's the thing, men, you can go from being the forgiven to then, over time, forgetting what you received and sliding into the heart of the older brother. You must stay on guard against this! Never forget the grace that welcomed you. We don't wallow in our past sin, but neither do we forget it and become self-righteous. The Apostle Paul is a great example of living in the confidence of his salvation while simultaneously knowing he was "the chief of sinners." He never forgot who he was when the Lord found him. He rightly saw himself as the worst of sinners, without giving in to pity or pride. Humble confidence that always celebrates radical grace being poured out on humble repentance is the road of spiritual vitality. Stay on guard against a self-righteous, cynical, critical spirit!

6 THE JOY OF SALVATION

There's nothing sweeter than coming "home." The Bible tells us that the joy of the Lord is our strength (Nehemiah 8:10). Stronger Men know the joy of salvation and celebrate forgiveness and salvation with the joy of Heaven. Grumbling, greed, and entitlement will creep into the forgetful heart. Practicing regular gratitude and generosity are the antidotes to grumbling, entitlement, and greed. Wield it daily. "*Give thanks to the Lord for He is good, His love endures forever*" (**Psalm 136**). "*Restore unto me the joy of my salvation. And renew a right spirit within me*" (**Psalm 51:12**). "*Repent that times of refreshing may come from the Lord*" (**Acts 3:19**). On the other side of repentance is sweet and refreshing joy. There is rest for your soul in the path of repentance and there is rest at your Father's table. His invitation to us is, "Come more often and stay longer." Remember the joy of forgiveness and be generous to extend it quickly to others.

7 THE MISSION OF JESUS AND THE CHRISTIAN LIFE

Be on the lookout for your lost brothers. Invite them home. Remind them of the goodness of the Father's house. Compel them to come in. Go out to bring them in. Welcome them in. Follow Jesus in the life of mission. As my good friend and Pastor Josh McPherson says often, "No one has more fun than Christians on mission." There's nothing like a front row seat to a brother coming home to the Lord and seeing the healing and restoring love of the Father, the power of grace, wash over a weary soul. The burdens lift, the sadness flees, the light returns to the eyes, and the awe and wonder of life are renewed. And the family heals and grows.

> Stronger men run home to the Father and help other lost sons and brothers do the same.

LET'S PRAY

Father, thank You for running to meet us on the way. Thank You for grace. Jesus, thank You for seeking me out and for laying down Your life and paying the price for my sin. Teach us to live with a heart of repentance and gratitude and to never lose the joy of our salvation. Holy Spirit, thank You for bringing me to my senses and drawing me home to the Father.

FROM A STRONGER MAN

When I was six, I was locked in a closet and left there for hours in the dark.

When I was 12, I was kicked out for the first time. It's also the first time I remember my father hitting me.

When I was 16 I was sent to a boarding school in Iowa that has since been shut down by the FBI. I was there for a year and a half and had to ask permission to walk through doorways, sit on the floor, or scratch an itch. Everything about my life was rigorously controlled. In order to get through it, I shoved all the anger down—feeling like I'd been sold off to be someone else's problem. I was angry that my dad couldn't figure out how to be a dad and actually step into the chaos and help me.

A few years later, I joined the U.S. Army and a number of things happened that challenged my relationship with God. One of my bunkmates in basic training hung himself in the stairwell, and I found his body. Both of my grandfathers and one of my closest friends all died in the same year.

After the end of my service contract, I met a gal and we got married. After two years of marriage, we had our first child who had a stroke when he was born and had to be resuscitated numerous times before we were flown to a hospital in Seattle.

Long story short, all the crap I'd been shoving down for years exploded out of me like a grenade in a dumpster full of dirty diapers.

My marriage, which wasn't great, pretty much stopped existing.

I openly mocked my wife Lacey for praying, especially over our son. *Oh, God's real, all right. But He can't possibly be good. If it were me, the NICU wouldn't exist. Children's hospitals wouldn't be a thing.*

I know better. I know pain. Look at all that I've been through and survived on my own. Where was Jesus when my dad was hurting me? Where was He when my friend was dying of muscular dystrophy at 10 years old? Where was He when Zach hung himself in the stairwell? Where was He when my dad told me he didn't love me?

WHERE IS HE NOW?

He's just like my earthly father: something for other people, lost to me.

Fast forward to the Stronger Man Nation Conference in 2022. Pastor Josh McPherson gave a challenge to do one of three things: apologize to your dad, forgive your dad, or thank your dad.

I started with my father-in-law, Norris. I drove straight to his house. A few other people were there but I pulled him aside and said, "I'm sorry, I feel like I'm the worst thing that's ever happened to your daughter. I don't deserve it, but can you forgive me?"

He said, "I've been waiting for this for a long time. You're already forgiven bro." And he hugged me like the prodigal son, finally home.

That feeling of his arms around me is tattooed on my brain. I'll never forget it.

Like my Grandpa, who earned two purple hearts in WWII—one in Normandy and one in Bastogne—it was time for me to assault the largest enemy stronghold in my life.

Nine days after the Stronger Man Nation Conference, I called my dad on my way to work. I didn't even know I was going to do it until it happened. As though he'd been waiting for it (and I found out later that he had been waiting for me to call for years), he picked up before the second ring. We talked for about 5 minutes.

I forgave him free and clear. I didn't want that hurt and anger any more. I didn't want to be that little boy locked in the closet anymore.

My youngest sister called me crying a day or two later. She said our dad called her and apologized for everything. I told her I was sorry I didn't do it sooner.

Since then, he has met his grandkids. He flew across the country to meet my wife and kids, and we flew to him, so my kids could see where I grew up. We ate together, flew kites, and stayed up late talking.

It was everything I ever wanted. Beneath all the anger and pain, I never stopped wanting my dad to show up. And in those moments, I looked back and saw that Jesus was always with me.

As a dad, my life and perspective has radically changed. I no longer abdicate my responsibilities. I read the Bible out loud every day. We pray as a family,

FROM A STRONGER MAN

we play as a family, we win and lose and celebrate and cry as a family. There is no space between us. The crumbling walls that I neglected—that were letting in evil and despicable things—have been remade and are stronger than ever.

My dad and I try to talk at least once a week. He's a part of my life, my kids' lives. I wept praying for that.

Jesus was always with me. He was with my dad, too. All along, Jesus was slowly changing him, preparing his heart for the day I'd finally call and ask him to be my dad again.

David, 34

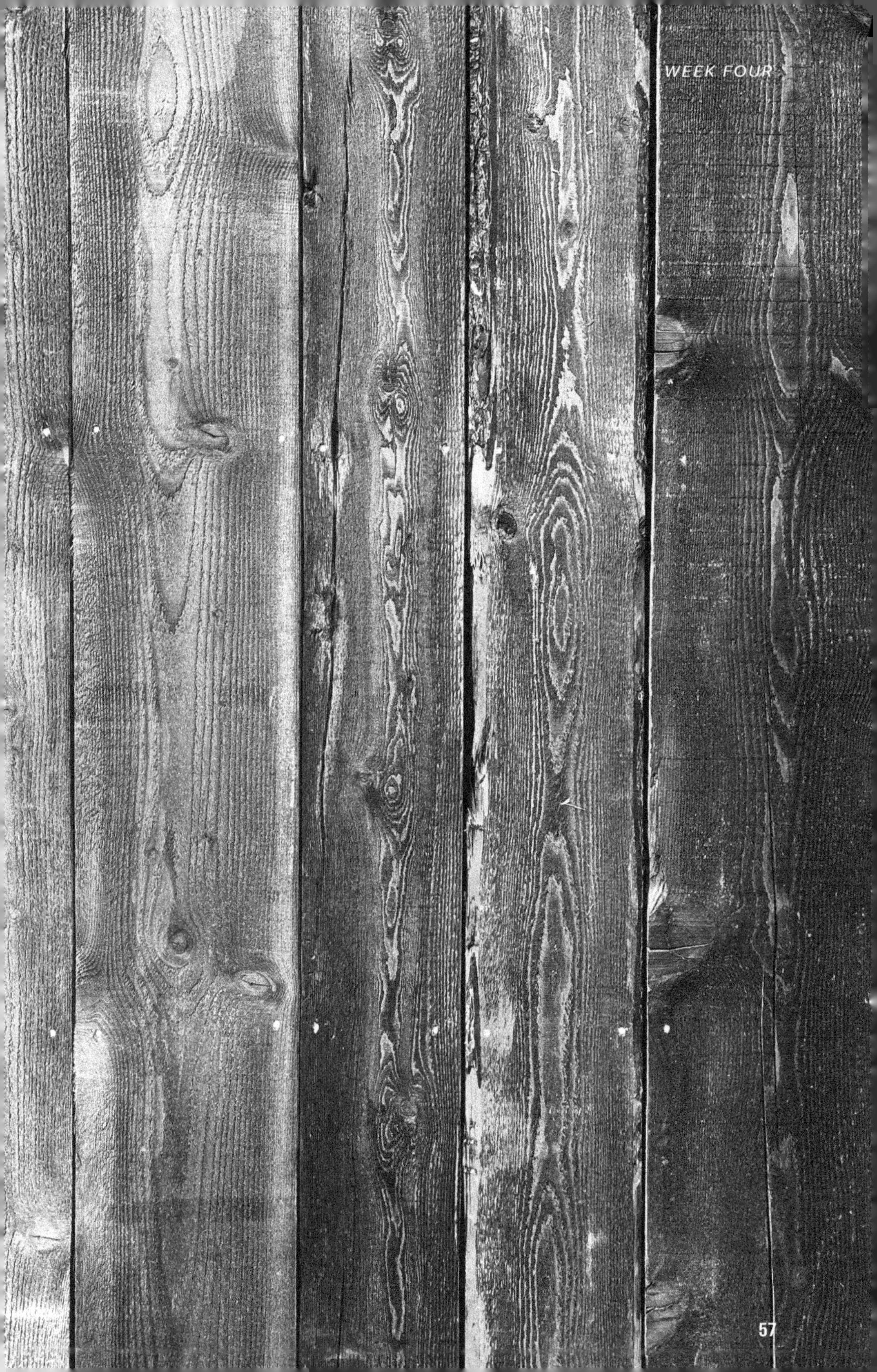

REFLECT & DISCUSS

1. What is your biggest takeaway from this chapter? What stood out to you as you read?

_____

_____

_____

2. In what ways do you identify with both the younger and older brothers? Which one do you most identify with?

_____

_____

_____

3. How have you experienced "coming to your senses" in your story? How would you describe your experience(s) of being humbled and brought to repentance?

_____

_____

_____

4. How would you describe being forgiven by God? Are you confident you're forgiven? And if so, what was that realization and experience like?

_____

_____

_____

5. Have you ever struggled with being "offended by grace?" What does the older brother in the story need to know and believe in order to respond rightly?

_____

_____

_____

6. What does this parable teach us about the heart of the Father?

_____

_____

_____

7. Which of the 7 Truths do you need to remember most right now in your life?

_____

_____

_____

TAKE ACTION

- Is there anything lingering in your mind and heart that you have not confessed to the Lord? Any sin that you are not fully sure has been forgiven? Make a list and, in your mind, hand it to the Father. What does He do with the list? What does He say to you in response? Picture the Father running to you. Receive His forgiveness.

- Is there any lingering anger, offense, or unforgiveness that you are harboring toward another person? What would it look like for you to release that person and that offense and give it to the Lord?

- Who are you praying for that you want to see come home to the Father? Write those names on a card or piece of paper and carry it with you this week to remind you to continue to pray for them.

WEEK 5

ADOPTED: SONS NOT SLAVES

But when the fullness of time had come, God sent forth His Son, born of woman, born under the law, to redeem those who were under the law, **AND BECAUSE YOU ARE SONS,** God has sent the Spirit of his Son into our hearts, crying, "Abba! Father!" So you are no longer a slave, but a son, and if a son, then an heir through God.

GALATIANS 4:4-7

FOR ALL WHO ARE LED BY THE SPIRIT OF GOD ARE SONS OF GOD. For you did not receive the spirit of slavery to fall back into fear, but you have received the Spirit of adoption as sons, by whom we cry, "Abba! Father!" The Spirit Himself bears witness with our spirit that we are children of God.

ROMANS 8:14-16

Praise be to the God and Father of our Lord Jesus Christ, who has blessed us in the heavenly realms with every spiritual blessing in Christ. For He chose us in Him before the creation of the world to be holy and blameless in His sight. **IN LOVE HE PREDESTINED US FOR ADOPTION TO SONSHIP THROUGH JESUS CHRIST,** in accordance with His pleasure and will— to the praise of His glorious grace, which He has freely given us in the One He loves.

EPHESIANS 1:3-6

Stronger men, through faith in Jesus Christ, are adopted sons of the Father, not abandoned slaves of the enemy.

This is the deepest and highest blessing of the gospel of Jesus Christ. The most potent truth. The most explosive promise. The most disruptive and, simultaneously, stabilizing reality in all of Christianity.

God wants all men to experience and embrace this truth with all their heart, mind, soul, and strength. The enemy opposes this with all his effort.

I repeat, the enemy hates that I'm writing this and that you're reading this. He will attempt to distract you. He will tempt you to be too hurried or too busy to absorb the truth of these words. He will attempt to discourage you or cause you to doubt. Resist him! Lean in and listen up. Take to heart the truth of God's Word.

Stronger men, in Christ, are fully loved sons who live for their good and gracious Father in Heaven.

You, my friend, are chosen and free. You once were orphaned by sin, cut off and floundering in the endless search for identity in a world that offers no solid ground. But then, God reached down and opened your ears and called your name. He gave His one and only Son, Jesus Christ, to die on the cross for your sins, so that you could be welcomed in as His adopted son to the praise of His glorious grace.

And He sent His Holy Spirit to cause that objective truth to land on your heart with subjective experiential power.

It's not true because you experience it. Rather, you can experience it because it's true.

The Spirit Himself testifies with our spirit that we are in fact, sons of God.

It's the single greatest, game-changing truth available to the Christian.

The highest and most glorious truth given to us in the gospel of Jesus Christ—the pinnacle blessing of the gospel—is the truth of our spiritual adoption as beloved sons of the Father.

Every man needs and craves this blessing.

It's the lifeblood and launchpad of every Stronger Man.

It both anchors and propels men into the calling of manhood.

Without it, we drift into the rocks. We sink into the abyss. And we pull anyone within reach down with us. There's just no escaping the negative impact of a man who doesn't know he's a loved son of the Father. And there's no denying the relief and freedom that flows from every masculine soul that beholds and believes the great promise of gospel adoption.

You may need to read this chapter twice—even if you've heard it before and know it to be true. The most veteran follower of Jesus among us has barely begun to enjoy the blessings and benefits of the glory of our adoption as sons of the Father.

Let's take a look at just a few of The Blessings and Benefits of Adoption:

ACCEPTANCE VS. ALIENATION

In Christ, you are fully accepted and no longer alienated from the life of God.

Ephesians 2:18-19 says, "*For through (Jesus) we both (Jews & Gentiles) have access to the Father by one Spirit. Consequently, you are no longer foreigners and aliens, but fellow citizens with God's people and members of God's household.*"

Follow the progression. You're no longer foreigners (far off), you're not even aliens (here but don't belong), you're now fellow citizens (here legally and you belong), but even more than that, you are members of God's household (here not just legally but loved)! You have ultimate access to the blessings and benefits of being God's child. You are fully accepted and welcomed into the most intimate access possible. A note of clarity: this does not mean God accepts ongoing sin. I am not speaking about the modern notion that "God accepts me as I am" with no expectation of repentance and the tacit approval of sinful choices or lifestyles. As a Christian, your life is now hidden with Christ in God. Positionally, you have a secure place in God's family. Volitionally, we must continue to fight sin, repent of sin, and grow in our obedience and faith in relationship with the Lord. But the good news of the gospel is that when we do sin, we are not cut off. We have been accepted and secured in Christ. We demonstrate this genuine reality by our ongoing battle against our own sin.

APPROVAL VS. ABANDONMENT

In Christ, you have the approval of the Father (we'll unpack this more in the next chapter). Contrast this full-hearted fatherly approval with

Satan's lie of abandonment. You are not abandoned. You are approved in Christ. The Father is pleased with you and He will never leave you nor forsake you.

AFFIRMATION VS. ACCOMPLISHMENT-DEPENDENT

There is power in the affirmation of the Father—words that build up and fill the soul with confidence. Affirmation anchors our soul. To be armed as a loved son, regardless of our performance or accomplishment is a stabilizing blessing that a conditional, performance-based, accomplishment-dependent relationship can never attain. Am I loved? Did I do enough? How will dad react this time? What does dad really think of me? These questions all get put to rest in the soul of the man who knows the power of affirmation that comes with the blessing of spiritual sonship and adoption. This too we will look at further in the next chapter.

AFFECTION VS. APATHY

God is not indifferent toward His children. He is not passive or apathetic in His expressions of His love and kindness toward His sons. He speaks with genuine affection. He embraces with hands both strong and tender. He wants face time with His boys. He loves His sons. Stronger Men can show appropriate and genuine, free-flowing affection toward their sons, fathers, brothers, daughters, mothers, and wives, because they've received the affection and warmth of their heavenly Father. A fist bump, a hand on the shoulder, a pat on the back, a full throttled hug, a kiss on the forehead, two hands on the shoulders, both hands on the face...eye-to-eye, heart engaged, intentional words, appropriate touch. Stronger Men can give and receive fatherly and brotherly affection.

ASSURANCE VS. ANXIETY

Theologians call the experience of spiritual adoption "the blessing of assurance." Without it, fear, doubt, worry, anxiety, and loneliness lurk in the shadows of the mind and heart. But God promised and poured out

His Holy Spirit, the Spirit of sonship, the Spirit by which we cry out, "Abba, Father!" So that we could know, with supernatural assurance, that we are in fact children of God. "The Spirit himself testifies with our spirit, that we are children of God." That's the Word of God telling us that the Holy Spirit will remind us that we are truly the loved and secure sons of God. This blessing of assurance is the sweetest gift that calms and comforts and lifts the soul like nothing else on planet Earth.

Here's my encouragement to you: if you do not yet have the blessing of this assurance, do not stop praying, reading, and asking the Holy Spirit to make the love of God real in your heart. Ask, seek, and knock. As we'll see in a few chapters, God is a good Father who loves to give good gifts to those who ask, especially the Holy Spirit. The blessing of assurance is a blood-bought promise to everyone who comes to the Father through the Son. Take Him at His Word and wrestle with God until He releases it into your heart.

Don't be deceived. Your soul craves these blessings and benefits.

Little children want their dad. It's unavoidable. And you are no exception.

You were given a great gift if you received these blessings from your earthly dad to point you to the goodness of your heavenly Father. Your growth as a boy was negatively impacted if you didn't receive these gifts from your earthly dad, but you've not been left as an orphan.

Even if you received these blessings from a mother, without the affirmation of a father, your soul will keep searching. In our natural sinful state, we will seek for that affirmation and acceptance in all the wrong places. Welcome to the junkyard of manly brokenness and destruction. Every addiction, every outburst, every idol is a sign of the soul's search for the love of God.

Whether you had an earthly dad or strong male figure in your life who demonstrated these qualities to you or not, your soul was created to receive these blessings directly from God Himself.

The day you discover this and experience the truth of it for the first time, not just in your mind, but with your heart, is the first day of the rest of your life. And the invitation is to walk in the light of that love and affirmation and bring it with you into every relationship and interaction from here forward.

The deepest part of a man needs to know he is loved by the Father. And when he does, it changes everything. He carries himself

with newfound freedom, confidence, rest, security, courage, compassion, and joy.

Augustine famously said, "Our hearts are restless until they find their rest in Thee, O God." And it has held true through all times. We're on a search to know we're wanted, known, and loved.

The toughest, hardest, and baddest dudes crumble under the love of the Father. Often, the reason they're tough, hard, and bad in the first place is because they don't know the love of the Father. The internal void and longing is what drives male anger, destructive hatred, and the defiance of authority that many men express. It's driven by the pain of rejection and the attempted denial of the subterranean reality of a fractured soul.

When you realize you are seen, known, loved, and chosen by God, the healing power of God's love can go to work rewiring your soul— even redeeming your broken past.

In this blessing of spiritual adoption, God's Spirit is poured out upon your heart. In an instant, you know you belong to God and that He loves you. You realize you really are His and He really is yours. You really do have His attention. He really does care. And you're blown away by the revelation that He knows everything about you—your deepest fear, your greatest desire—and still, He loves you.

Your soul glitches under the weight of that glory and knowledge. You may even fall to your knees and weep. The Holy Spirit comes upon you and relays the truth to your heart that you are in fact a child of God. A loved son. A chosen son. An adopted son. God is your Father and He is for you, with you, over you, and sends His Spirit, the Spirit of adoption, to dwell within you, by which your soul cries out, "Abba, Father!"

Our Father's presence is the greatest place in the seen and unseen realm.

Furthermore, nothing comes into your life except that which has been sifted through the hands of your perfect Father. He has provided everything you will need for total healing, strong faith, joy in the midst of sorrow, hope in the midst of despair, and light for your path in the midst of darkness. He begins to tune your spiritual ear to His voice.

It is both objective and subjective truth for the Christian. You may not always feel it, but it is always true for those who have given their lives to Christ. You may need to taste it or touch it in a new or deeper way, but you can ask, seek, and knock for the Lord to grant you the gift of that deep, abiding assurance that you are His.

You're not the center of the universe. Yet, in Christ, God's love is set upon you. Salvation is more than having your sins forgiven. It's more than the gift of eternal life. It's more than freedom from guilt and shame. It's the fundamental transformation of your deepest identity from slave to son. From orphaned to adopted.

God wanted you in His family and He did all the work necessary to secure the reality of that happening.

Do you have this assurance? Which blessing and benefit of adoption do you need to believe today?

LET'S PRAY

Father, I thank You that we can call You Father. That You hear us. That You see us. That You know us. That You love us. That You have adopted us as Your sons by faith in Your Son, Jesus. Pour out Your Holy Spirit upon my brother reading this. Blow away any dust on the surface of his soul. Fan into flame the reality of Your presence in his life. Chip away at any defenses that remain in place. Speak his name and call him to Yourself in undeniable and irresistible grace. Show him what he needs to see. Tell him what he needs to hear. According to the truth of Your Word, anchor him in the truth of his sonship and lead him into the fiery furnace of Your love for him. Break down and break through any and every resistance. Cut off the lies of the enemy. Heal the wounds of unfaithful fathers. Show us our place at Your table. In Jesus' Name, amen.

FROM A STRONGER MAN

I grew up in small-town Wisconsin. My mom was an ER nurse. My dad owned a small business and delivered mail. Our home was the place my friends gathered. My mom cooked for everyone. My dad allowed his boys to be boys. My older brother and I competed in everything, which usually ended in fights. My dad's parents started the first southeastern Wisconsin pizza tavern in 1954. I grew up in the tavern with a wild mullet, bussing tables, crushing beer cans, and sweeping the bar floor for tips. Weaving through drunks was the norm on any given Saturday night at the tavern.

As a teenager, my identity was forged by sports. I pridefully veered away from drinking because of what I saw at the tavern. Additionally, I did not value the church or my sonship. Church felt feminized and forced, and obeying my parents was not a priority. Sports gave me a platform to compete, justify myself, and flaunt. My shallow identity in sports drove me to play college basketball. The pride that prevented me from drinking, eventually pushed me to drink. After two years of college, I quit the basketball team, dropped out, started drinking heavily, and worked just enough warehouse hours to pay for my habits. These habits grew from social drinking to isolated drinking to drugs to much worse. At 24, I was a pathetic boy: multiple addictions, part-time work, partying, lying, bumming on couches, and searching for worth in superficial relationships.

In the spring of 2009, while living in Oshkosh, WI, I went back home to see my brother. We debated about God. I believed in Universalism. He believed in Jesus. To end the debate, he handed me his Bible and challenged me to read the Gospels. I accepted the challenge to prove him wrong. For the next couple months, in drunk and high stupors, I read the Gospels. In the process of trying to discredit my brother's faith, God saved me.

No church building. No white-knuckled effort. No pastor. No serving Him. No exalting Him.

The Holy Spirit convicted me of my sin in light of a holy God. He showed me clearly, through His Word, that Jesus holds the only key to eternal life. My shallow identity withered. God's kindness brought me to my knees that summer morning in Oshkosh. I repented of my sins and became born-again by God's Spirit, not by my effort.

By God's grace, I quit drinking, drugs, and eventually graduated from college. In 2012, I felt prompted to journey west from Wisconsin. I packed up the car, hit I-90, and ran into a port city called Tacoma, Washington. For the first time, I plugged into a church body, got baptized, and worked honest jobs. Through the local church, I learned more about my heavenly Father and who

I am in His family. The Gospel produces many things within a man and revelation of sonship is one of the most important. The deeper God took me in His Word, the more passionate I became about the Father being my Father and how He is Father to the fatherless.

At the end of 2014, I left Tacoma and drove cross country to invest in troubled youth in Pike County, Georgia. Some of the youth I discipled were orphans from war-torn countries, which sparked a strong desire to serveorphansoverseas.In2016, through God-ordained circumstances, I left Georgia and jetted to the Busia District of Uganda, Africa where I planted Biblical curriculum in schools and started orphan support programs for the fatherless. God multiplied my time in Uganda by establishing a nonprofit organization called "Son Mission"—which has been serving orphans with education and discipleship since 2016. Son Mission is fueled by Paul's writings in Romans 8:14-17. The testimonies of spiritual and physical orphans finding sonship in Christ are abundant!

In 2017, I was back stateside. I embarked on another cross country journey, back to Washington for a job to counsel incarcerated boys for the State. God planted me in a flourishing local church where I found my wife and lifelong brothers in Christ. I quickly discovered that Ugandan orphans and incarcerated boys have this in common: no fathers. Part of my work involved reconciling these incarcerated boys to their families, which was futile because dads weren't present. I built re-entry plans for 100+ boys in five years. Three out of 100+ dads played a role in re-entry for their sons. Only three.

In 1969, my dad was 19 when he enlisted in the Army to serve in the Vietnam War. While stationed in Fort Campbell, he was notified that his dad died of a sudden heart attack. The point is this: all our dads have a story with their dads and these stories play a vital role in our story with our dads and how we see our heavenly Father. It is easy to see the failings of my earthly father (and myself as a father) in light of my heavenly Father. I believe that's the point. **The hero of all our stories is Jesus, not our dads. The more I dive into God's Word the more I see the profound love between God the Father and God the Son, and how that love transforms me as a son and father.** I still have the Bible my brother gave in the summer of 2009 as a reminder of the legacy-changing power in God's Word. It is by grace alone that a mullet boy in a smoke-filled tavern from the sticks of Wisconsin would have the opportunity to forge a legacy of faith for his children.

Logan, 39

REFLECT & DISCUSS

1. What is your biggest takeaway from this chapter? What stood out to you as you read?

_____

_____

_____

2. Many men struggle to talk about these things. Why do you think that is?

_____

_____

_____

3. How have you experienced the blessings and benefits of spiritual adoption?

_____

_____

_____

4. How were acceptance, approval, affirmation, affection, and assurance modeled or missing in your home growing up?

_____

_____

_____

5. What are some of the results in a man's soul when he does not have the assurance of the love of a father and, ultimately, the Father?

_____

_____

_____

6. What are the signs that show up in your life when you've forgotten or are not walking in the power of your sonship in Christ?

_____

_____

_____

7. What is the fruit in your relationships when you bring the presence and assurance that you are an adopted, free, loved son? How does receiving and believing this truth of the gospel impact your ability to connect and relate with others?

_____

_____

_____

TAKE ACTION

Create moments and opportunities to express these 5 Blessings and Benefits of Adoption to your family and friends this week. Use intentional words, meaningful eye contact, and appropriate touch to convey to those around you your love and God's love for them.

WEEK 6

THE FATHER'S BLESSING

As soon as Jesus was baptized, He went up out of the water. At that moment Heaven was opened, and He saw the Spirit of God descending like a dove and alighting on Him. And a voice from Heaven said,

'THIS IS MY SON, WHOM I LOVE; WITH HIM I AM WELL PLEASED.'

MATTHEW 3:16-17

Few things in the Bible carry more weight than a father's blessing.

The favor of God is bestowed through blessing: Identity. Affirmation. Approval. Inheritance. Legacy.

A father's blessing is a multifaceted concept in Scripture, encompassing spiritual, relational, and cultural benefits. Provision, land, inheritance, protection, spiritual authority, identity, well-being, and family legacy were all a part of this blessing. It serves as a means of transferring God's promises, guidance, identity, and well-being to the next generation.

The father is the head of the family. He will either set that family on a trajectory of blessing or cursing. He has no vote in whether or not he is the head. He is, by the mere fact that his role is assigned by God. It is inescapable. The question is not whether or not he will be the head, but what kind of head he will be. As head, the father carries the spiritual authority that is unique and profound in its impact and purpose.

God calls men to protect, provide, lead, and love. A father's blessing encompasses every one of those components.

A man's leadership in his home is not to be conducted with a heavy-handed pronouncement that, "I'm in charge!" Rather, it's a weight he carries carefully, knowing his words carry power, knowing his attitude sets the tone, knowing his affirmation touches a place in the soul of his family that nothing else and no one else can. He's been given that role and responsibility by God. How he conducts himself will be the single greatest factor in the health of that household. Whenever and however he needs to exercise his God-given authority, he is always to do so with a heart of love.

The New Testament makes this abundantly clear. As men, we are to follow the example of Jesus in how we lay down our lives in sacrificial love and service. In marriage, we are to live with our wives in an understanding way and to lay down our lives as leaders who serve, protect, and bless with our words and actions.

As husbands and fathers, we are not dictators. We are lovers. We bring and give blessing.

The redemptive story of the Bible is carried along from generation to generation through the covenant promises of God transmitted through fathers blessing the next generation—from Abraham, to Isaac, to Jacob. Jacob became 'Israel' and had 12 sons who became the 12 tribes of Israel, one of whom was Judah, through whom eventually came the Messiah and Savior of the world, the Lord Jesus Christ. At each point of transition, the blessing from a father conferred the favor of God on the next generation.

Notably, the parts of the Bible that seem the most boring, the lists of names of descendants and the lineage of Israel, carry great importance as you trace the covenant line of blessing that would ultimately bring us Jesus, "in whom all the nations of the earth will be blessed."

Even in the most dysfunctional of families, as the family of the patriarchs most certainly was, this role of a father giving his blessing, and the significance ascribed to it, casts a long shadow.

In Genesis 27, we read the story of Isaac blessing Jacob. This blessing was so important and so significant that Jacob deceived his father, with his mother's help, to receive the blessing instead of his brother Esau. Esau was Isaac's favorite—for the record, having favorites never goes well—as he was a man of the field, a skilled hunter. A man's man who could grow a mean, red beard. Jacob, on the other hand liked to stay by the tents. He was a mama's boy with smooth skin and was a deceiver from birth.

But God had said, "The older (Esau) will serve the younger (Jacob)," and even though deception was involved, Isaac's blessing carried great importance in continuing the covenant promises that God had given Abraham. God promised to make Abraham into a great nation and, through his family, bless all the nations of the earth. The Lord had already chosen this blessing to come through Jacob, not Esau.

The providence of God is seen through a father's blessing, even in the wild family drama that can unfold. The father's blessing is a big, big deal.

Earlier in the story, Esau had foolishly despised and sold his birthright to Jacob for a pot of stew. And now, the father's blessing fell to Jacob, as well. Even though Esau sought for it with tears, it could not be retracted. This led to great anger, a deep grudge, and a fractured relationship between the brothers. But it also paved the way for a scene of sweet reconciliation between the brothers later in life.

The fact remains, Jacob received his father's blessing. Esau did not.

The difference rolled out in both men's lives and continued to cascade down generations beneath them.

So it is with men today. There are transferable principles that play out in every family.

When blessing is withheld by a father, it scars a son deeply. Many sons are still searching for their father's blessing. Without it, men can be driven to do the craziest things. There's no amount of discipline, achievement, accomplishment, money, or success that can replace a father's blessing. No amount of anger, bitterness, revenge, or bloodshed satisfies it either. Without a father's blessing, there simply remain unanswered questions in a man's soul that will stay with him into his old age and death bed. Or, tragically and selfishly, these scars can even cause men to take their own lives.

Brothers, listen. It's that powerful. God made it to be so.

Life and death are in the power of the tongue. The words of a father are filled with power. For blessing or cursing. Given or withheld.

With a father's blessing, men can pursue great heights. They are free to do so with a sense of abiding peace and approval, knowing they have their father's blessing. This can powerfully propel a son to pursue greatness for all the right reasons. To make their life count in the service of God's Kingdom for the good of others.

So now comes the question: have you received your father's blessing?

Do you know you have received it? How do you know? What do you do if you haven't?

And, if you're a dad reading this, will you give your sons and daughters the gift of a father's blessing? How do you do that? What does that look like?

Here's the challenge: you can't truly give what you don't possess. To give a blessing, you must first receive a blessing. To draw a bucket of water, you have to have a well that isn't empty to draw from.

But what if your dad's no longer around? What if he's already passed away? Or has no interest or ability to give you his blessing? There's a good chance he never got his father's blessing either. So what do we do?

Enter the power of the gospel. Enter **Matthew 3:16-17**:

> *And a voice from Heaven said, "This is my Son, whom I love; with Him I am well pleased."*

Jesus received this blessing from His Father, publicly, at His baptism. Before He had preached a sermon or performed a miracle, He had His Father's blessing.

His identity was secure. He was greatly loved by the pure fact of His sonship, unrelated to His performance or accomplishment. He was powerfully armed and fully accepted.

Jesus knew His Father loved Him. Jesus knew His Father was proud of Him.

It was at this very moment that the Spirit came upon Jesus like a dove from Heaven and empowered Him to live in the fullness of God's blessing and calling on His life.

The Spirit and blessing of sonship gave Him an anchor to endure the storm of temptation that followed in the desert. It sustained Him in times He was tired and exhausted. When He was outnumbered and surrounded. When He was opposed and falsely accused. Even when He was betrayed, mocked, beaten, and ultimately, crucified for the very sinners who were rejecting Him.

The Father's blessing was an important affirmation of the identity of Jesus Christ as the unique Son of God. And it was also a pronouncement of blessing on all those who place their faith in Christ, are identified with Jesus, and adopted as sons of the Father.

Jesus is the Eternally Blessed Firstborn Son. When you repent of your sins and trust in Jesus Christ, you are brought into and under the Father's blessing.

As followers of Jesus, we are now sons of God. Our life is now found "in Christ." In Christ, the Father sees you and declares His love, affirmation, and approval over you. In Christ, your identity is secure. Your sonship is armed.

How great is the love the Father has lavished on us, that we should be called children of God! And that is what we are! **1 John 3:1**

Whether you received your father's blessing or not, you have access to a better blessing from God when you become a child of God through faith in Jesus.

His blessing is unconditional. Before you do a single thing, He is pleased and proud. He has set His love upon you because you are His son. And you are His son because your life is now wrapped up in His one and only Son, Jesus Christ.

In Christ, your hope is found. In Christ, you are wrapped in His righteousness as a free gift of grace. In Christ, you are covered in His blood, and your guilt is removed. In Christ, you died to your old life of sin and rose to a new life of obedience by the power of the Holy Spirit. In Christ, the Father is also pleased with you, not because of what you have or haven't done, but because of what Jesus has already done.

In Christ, you are eternally affirmed and sufficiently approved. In Christ, God is for you. You never have to wonder again.

In Christ, you are sheltered from the accusations of the evil one.

When you receive the Father's blessing, you receive a greater blessing than any earthly father could give, and you are now able to bless your sons and daughters from an overflow of His blessing.

How? You **speak words** of affirmation over them. You look them in the eye, you tell them you love them, you tell them you're proud of them. You embrace them and pray for them.

And as they grow and prepare to launch, you keep blessing them.

And before you die, if God gives you the opportunity to have them around your bed, you bless them.

At key moments of their life, you bless them.

At times of transition, at birthdays, at holidays, you bless them.

Let there be no doubt. Let there be no question. Write it down. Speak it over them. Privately and publicly, bless them with words of love.

But it's not just mere words. They must come from a sincere and authentic place of integrity. They must be intentional, meaningful, heartfelt, thoughtful words of blessing. Seek the help of the Holy Spirit who wants to give you specific words for each of your children.

Furthermore, if you have opportunity, you can even bless your own father, with words he may not have received himself. You can forgive him. You can thank him. You can honor him.

There is grace and healing and power and security available that can start a new family line of blessing instead of cursing.

If you are a Christian reading this and have never been baptized as a follower of Jesus, I encourage you to take that step of obedience. Your baptism is not just *your* declaration to the world that you now belong to God and that Jesus is your Savior and Lord. We often hear baptism described primarily or only as the declaration of the one being baptized. And, certainly, that is an important and powerful aspect of what is happening. But may I submit to you that above and beyond that, is the declaration of the Father, "This is My son, whom I love, in whom I am well pleased!"

In your baptism, the Father is declaring His love for you. The Father is saying, 'This one is Mine. He belongs to Me. He's My beloved son and he has My blessing, My protection, My provision, My leading, and My love set upon him. I am his and he is Mine.'

In Christ, you have identified with the firstborn Son of the living God and you have been immersed in the blessing of the Father.

How should that change the way you live today? How should it change the way you love and lead your family? How should it affect the words you use to bless your sons and daughters?

Stronger Men walk in the blessing of the Father, as securely loved sons, and bless their wives and children with Spirit-born words of power.

LET'S PRAY

Father, I am again praying for my brother reading this. Open the eyes and ears of his sanctified imagination to hear Your love and affirmation over him. Speak to him now. Help him listen and hear. Your love for us is beyond words. Thank You, Jesus, for being the Way, the Truth, and the Life that brings us to the Father. Make us into Stronger Men who carry the blessing of our heavenly Father in the deepest part of our soul and can speak words of blessing over our families and over those You call us to serve and bless. Empower forgiveness and healing where needed. Give rest and peace where needed. In Jesus's Name, amen.

FROM A STRONGER MAN

MY BROKEN LINE

My story as a son does not follow a straight path and definitely diverges from God's design. Deep Christian roots would not describe my heritage, and men of faith do not go before me. Parts of my story are hard to share because hard things have happened—especially between my dad and I. It's been messy and complicated at times. There are aspects that aren't resolved. Conversations that aren't over, and things that still need to be done and said...and yet, I'm eager to share with you because God has intervened in my life and the story has taken a turn.

The facts are, my parents divorced when I was three. My dad remarried two more times and had two more divorces by the time I was 10. My mom remarried when I was eight and is still with my stepdad to this day. Their marriage is sweet and always has been. My stepdad is a good man, but he's also a hard man and doesn't know the Lord.

What little I knew of God, early on, I got from my mom who would take us to church on the big holidays—she taught me how to live a well-mannered, moral life and instilled a good and right fear through her discipline, but her faith was private and because my step dad wasn't a believer, God wasn't a focus for us as a family. There was no mention of Jesus or the good news of the gospel, nor of sin, forgiveness, grace, and mercy. I learned early on that religion and faith was personal, private, and mostly off limits.

So, I ran hard chasing many things, just not God. I was after sports, girls, my reputation, a future partnership in the construction business that my step dad owned, and my identity as someone who could perform well being a self-made man—finding my own version of a full life.

That's right where the heavenly Father met me, running hard in the wrong direction. Over the course of a few years, beginning my junior year of high school, God began to use some really challenging events to get my attention—trials I didn't have answers for—and they became the beginning of my end...and the beginning of a new me. I gave my life to Jesus in those years and began to walk in a new path.

WHEN I MET MY FATHER

I am a son, known and loved, with whom my Father is well pleased. Before I even leave to attack the day or the world, I am beloved. This is the truth that sealed my identity as a son and sparked something new in my family line.

It was my freshman year of college, I was brand new to my faith, but hungry for truth so I was in the Word constantly. One morning, I read the account of Jesus' baptism in

Matthew—this was the text:

> *As soon as Jesus was baptized, He went up out of the water. At that moment Heaven was opened, and He saw the Spirit of God descending like a dove and alighting on him. And a voice from Heaven said, "This is my Son, whom I love; with Him I am well pleased."*

I had also recently read in the letter to the Colossians about how the Christian's life is hidden in Christ; and in Romans, how if we live by the Spirit of God, then we are children of God. We are adopted as sons and get to call God our Father.

In that moment the Holy Spirit connected the dots for me—I get to share in the inheritance of Christ as a son. I get to hear, "This is my Son, whom I love; with him I am well pleased." Those words are for me, a son.

That truth changed everything, especially my relationships with my dad and stepdad. Not that it made everything easier—in some ways things have gotten harder. But now that I know the love of my heavenly Father and my identity as a son is secure, I can love my dad and stepdad without expectation—with patience and hope. Not that I've done this flawlessly, nor has all the hurt gone away, but I know my cup is full and so I'm free to meet them where they're at and I pray they each find the love of the Heavenly Father—for their sake, and for ours.

2 REASONS FOR HOPE

And wouldn't you know it, the broken kid who grew up with two broken dads would be given two sons—twin boys, in fact. God is funny. It's as if to say, "How about I flip this whole thing on its head? I'll soften the heart of your dads, you'll see, with two little boys that you'll raise with Me. I'll pass the torch of 'Dad' to you, and as My son, whom I love, you'll know what to do. Your dads will look on and over time they'll see, I'm using you and these boys to repair the family tree."

This is my hope and I'm trusting God for it. So, pray for my dad and my stepdad, my boys and me, that the gift of sonship would bring full unity and healing through Jesus.

Brian, 36

REFLECT & DISCUSS

1. What is your biggest takeaway from this chapter? What stood out to you as you read?

_____

_____

_____

2. Would you say you received your earthly father's blessing? If you're uncertain or if it's a mixed bag for you, in what ways would you say "yes" and in what ways would you say "no?"

_____

_____

_____

3. Why do you think a father's blessing is so important and impactful? How do you identify with the need and desire for a father's blessing?

_____

_____

_____

4. What questions does this chapter raise in your mind and heart?

_____

_____

_____

5. Have you been baptized as a follower of Jesus? If so, share your baptism story/experience. Had you ever thought about what the Father is saying and declaring over you at your baptism? Or was it mainly about your declaration as a follower of Jesus? How does that difference/addition impact your understanding of baptism?

_____

_____

_____

6. Why is it important that the blessing is "unconditional" and not dependent on anything that has been accomplished or earned? What does that say about what it is based on?

_____

_____

_____

7. What do you think God the Father wants you to hear Him say personally to you through the truth discussed in this chapter? Write down what you think He would say to you.

_____

_____

_____

TAKE ACTION

- Write a letter or note of blessing to each of your children. Based on where they currently are in life, ask the Lord to give you words of blessing and encouragement specific and personal for them. Make a plan to share it with them. Look for future opportunities to reference, repeat, or add to those words at key moments and events along the way (birthdays, milestones, anniversaries, important moments, etc).

- If you're not a father, write a letter or note of blessing to a sibling, friend, or key person in your life.

WEEK 7

OUR FATHER IN HEAVEN

But when you pray, go into your room, close the door and pray to your Father, who is unseen. Then your Father, who sees what is done in secret, will reward you. And when you pray, do not keep on babbling like pagans, for they think they will be heard because of their many words. Do not be like them, for your Father knows what you need before you ask Him. This, then, is how you should pray: 'OUR FATHER IN HEAVEN, HALLOWED BE YOUR NAME...'

MATTHEW 6:6-9

For those who place their faith in Jesus Christ, God is "Our Father in Heaven."

He is holy, holy, holy. He is the God above all gods, the Most High God, the Creator of all, who dwells in unapproachable light.

And yet, as Our Father, He is relational. Accessible. Available.

Theologians use words like "transcendent" and "immanent." He is both far above, holding stars in His hands, and is also nearer than your breath and can place His hand upon you.

One of the first realizations that came upon my mind and heart as the Lord was drawing me out of darkness and into His light, out of sin and into repentance, out of slavery and into freedom, was the simple fact that God is real. He is real and He is present. He knows me. He knows my thoughts. He knows my past, my present, and my future. Not one moment of my life has been or will ever be hidden from His sight.

And yet, He didn't throw in the towel. He didn't put me to death in my sins. He didn't walk away and remove His presence from me. Instead, He sent His Son. He drew near to me. He came knocking. He came revealing Himself as a loving, holy Father.

As the fear of the Lord came upon my heart, late at night in my apartment bedroom, I awoke to the reality that God, in fact, exists and was waiting for me to talk to Him. It was time to do business with God.

Somehow, I had been able to avoid that reality for 19 years. But there was no avoiding it any longer. I had to decide which way I was going to go. Who I was going to become. What I truly believed. And let it impact my life however it needed to.

I did not automatically surrender my life to God. There was a period of wrestling. But the internal pressure mounted as the external incongruence was exposed...I said I believed in God, but my life said otherwise.

A point of decision was brewing. In or out?

On one weekend trip home, I found an old Bible I had been given, snuck it in my bag, and brought it back to my apartment. Late at night, alone, with the door closed, I pulled it out, turned on my desk lamp, and like a thief pouring over stolen documents, began to read. And think. And read. And think.

My relationship with God began in secret. It began with the door closed. God was the one knocking on the door of my heart, and He was making it clear that He already knew me. He was inviting me to begin to get to know Him.

A few weeks of this went by before it finally broke the surface—my repentance and faith in Jesus became public. I confessed my sins, waved the white flag of surrender to Jesus, and began leaving my old life.

With new desires and new eyes, I began displaying new attitudes and new actions. Wobbly as I was, I was on a new path and my personal experience with God, alone in my room, was the charging station for this new life I was just beginning to live.

Even as our faith must inevitably become visible and public to be real, even as it must be on display with real fruit in our lives, the secret to the Christian life is still found in the unseen places. Just you and God. You and your heavenly Father.

There is no place for pretending or performing. The invitation is to be real. Not flippant. Not religious. Respectful and real.

In this secret, hidden chamber of a man's personal life with God, true spiritual life is born, fueled and sustained. A son with his Father.

For a tree to be healthy and bear good fruit, it is the part of the tree you can't see— the roots—that must be alive, active, and healthy.

When the roots are compromised, it is only a matter of time before the tree begins to die, the fruit ceases to grow, or the tree itself is blown over in a storm.

It is the unseen roots that give the tree its true life, strength, and stability.

So it is with a man and God. The unseen prayer life, the unseen conversations, the unseen surrender, worship, listening, and honesty are your source of strength and stability.

As a man is on his knees before God, and when he is alone with God, that is the truest picture of that man as he is.

When God finds a man who is willing to honor Him in private, it is safe for God to honor that man in public. The rewards of knowing God as your Father, and spending time with Him in secret, will eventually be evident for all to see. But that's never the motivation. It is merely the promise of God.

Hypocrisy always gets exposed. So does integrity. Jesus said in **Matthew 7:20**, "*You will know a tree by its fruit.*" The Father knows the difference between a fake, plastic tree with no roots and the real thing. Sometimes a good fake is hard to tell, but in the end, it always becomes known.

In a sobering warning, Jesus said, "*Not everyone who says to Me, 'Lord, Lord,' will enter the Kingdom of Heaven, but only he who does the will of My Father who is in Heaven. Many will say to Me on that day, 'Lord, Lord, did we not prophesy in Your Name, and in Your Name drive out demons and perform many miracles?' Then I will tell them plainly, 'I never knew you. Away from Me, you evil doers'*" (**Matthew 7:21-23**).

The genuineness of faith and of relationship with God results in a genuine life of service to God, both in outward action and internal motivation. The Father knows those who are truly His. When you pray, remember, you're talking to your Father in Heaven. He already sees, already knows, and wants the real you.

This is the inner chamber of the Christian life that we never leave behind. There's no graduating from the private school of secret prayer. This is the time and place we truly come to know that God is our Father and we are His loved sons. It's the time and place we return to again and again.

If God seems distant to you, let me encourage you to get alone with Him—with a Bible—ask Him to speak to you, to reveal Himself to you, to lead you into truth, and then spend time reading, thinking, listening, journaling, and praying. Don't just try it once and give up. Stay with it. Go again and again, until a personal experience and breakthrough comes. Once you've found that path, through Jesus, to the Father, you'll know how to keep going to Him. And then it can become a well-worn path that you spend the rest of your life walking. To the Father. Back to the Father. Alone with the Father.

I started in the Psalms. Then ended up in the Gospel of Mark. Then Romans. Then Ephesians. Then I read about the heroes of the faith I remember learning about as a child: Abraham, Joseph, Moses, Samson, David, Elijah, Daniel, Jonah, Peter, and Paul.

I used to be totally intimidated by the Bible and totally confused about how it all fit together and what it all meant. Then I read it! And it started to make sense. I had others who began to help me understand it and helped me connect the dots.

The more I read, the more I was blown away and convinced of the reality of God and His pursuit of me as a loving and holy Father.

This "personal relationship" with God unlocked the greatest joy, freedom, peace, strength, hope, comfort, confidence, humility, gratitude, and hunger for more of Him than I had ever known in my life.

This is the repeated testimony throughout history of men who have come to know Jesus as their Savior and Lord, and God as their Father, in the secret chamber of the soul.

Jesus taught His followers how to pray in this secret place, by giving them the pattern of prayer we know as "The Lord's Prayer."

It begins: "Our Father in Heaven, hallowed be Your Name."

It is not about a rote, rigid, recipe or recitation. It is about kindling the fire of revival in your soul, when no one else is there and you simply come as a hungry, dependent child, and talk to your heavenly Father.

It doesn't have to be long, and it doesn't have to be loud. There's nothing to prove and no one to impress. It just has to be real, with faith in the God who is there waiting.

Hebrews 11:6 says, "*Without faith it is impossible to please God, because anyone who comes to Him must believe that He exists and that He rewards those who earnestly seek Him.*"

Brother, your Father is waiting with reward in hand. Do not be deterred. Do not be delayed. You will not be denied.

Jesus said in **John 6:37**, "*All that the Father gives me will come to me, and whoever comes to me I will never drive away.*" And in **6:44**, "*No one can come to me unless the Father who sent me draws him, and I will raise him up at the last day.*"

Is the Father drawing you? Have you come to Jesus?

Spend time alone with the Father in secret, and watch the rest of your life story begin to unfold with the blessing of God as you live a life of real and revived faith.

Consider the following statements as we bring this chapter to a close:

→ Your relationship with your Father in Heaven is the most important relationship in your life.

→ The secret inner chamber of your heart, where you come to God as a trusting child, and stand fully known before Him, is the source of your confidence before the world.

→ Your Father knows, sees, and cares.

→ Your Father loves to see your face and hear your voice.

→ Your spiritual vitality is only as real and strong as your secret, unseen fellowship with the Father.

→ Your integrity is only as authentic in public as it is in private.

→ God can use a man greatly in public who honors Him earnestly in private.

→ There is no place for pretense or pretending when we come to God in prayer. Get real right away.

→ Through faith in Jesus, you can talk to God as though He is your perfect, loving, holy, heavenly Father, because He is.

This is the furnace of a Stronger Man's soul, the center of a God-glorifying life, marriage, family, church, or business; the starting place for a life set free to love.

LET'S PRAY

Father, thank You for drawing us to Yourself. Thank You for calling us by name. That while we were yet sinners, You sent Your Son to die on the cross for us. Even when we were hiding, wandering, wondering, or running, You came searching. You've known us all along. Thank You for inviting us to come to You, for making room for us at Your table, for always having room for us in Your "schedule." Thank You for being Our Father in Heaven. Help us honor You in private and public, as we do Your will each day, with integrity of heart, that we might bear good fruit as faithful sons. In Jesus' Name, amen.

FROM A STRONGER MAN

I grew up in a fatherless home. And even though my dad lived in the same city, he wasn't a regular in my life. He was absent, disengaged. I'd go weeks without seeing him. Then, after I moved out of the area as a young teenager, I'd go months without seeing him or even talking to him.

I have no recollection of talking with my dad about anything of substance. No memories of conversations about school, grades, trips, jobs, girls, politics, marriage, family, religion. Our conversations were, and still are, shallow. Surface-level. It's weather, movies, sports. Nothing about life or anything that really matters.

One interaction with my dad vividly stands out because it was the first time I realized the impact of my dad's absence on our relationship. I was 19 and getting married. It was such exciting news and yet I wasn't excited to tell him. And when I did, it felt more like I was talking with a neighbor. Someone you know of, maybe wave at from time to time, but don't really know. And here I am saying "dad," which is a very personal, relationally warm name, to someone that knows less about me than one of my high school teachers. It was oxymoronic, to say the least.

Now, throw in a mom who had all but checked out by the time I was 12, and my dominant emotional memories as an adolescent and young man were shame and loneliness. And that produced a suffocating amount of insecurity. I attempted to fix it all by chasing affirmation from friends and from girls. The more of each, the better. All of it led to stupid, foolish, gross, horrific sin. And none of it "fixed me."

But then, Jesus.

As a senior in high school, a Christian friend, who was one of the only Christians I had ever known, and I were talking during ceramics class (because that's where riveting conversations always happen, especially for those students needing an easy class to fulfill graduation requirements). I'm not sure why, but I started asking him all kinds of questions about Heaven. "Are the streets really paved with gold? Will people remember their life on earth?" I was genuinely curious.

The next day, this same friend walked up to me in the hallway at school and handed me a New Testament Bible. He didn't say much of anything. He just handed it to me and walked away.

That night, I opened the Bible. And I read. I read all of Jesus' miracles in each of the Gospels. Turning water into wine, walking on the sea, calming the storm, casting out demons, raising the dead to life. All His miracles. I wanted to know if Jesus is who He said He is. Then, I read the entire book of Revelation. I wanted to know what the Bible said about how it all ended. Life, the earth, good, evil. I didn't understand much of what I read (perhaps most of what I read), until I got to this verse:

> *I am the Alpha and the Omega, the Beginning and the End. To him who is thirsty I will give to drink without cost from the spring of the water of life. He who overcomes will inherit all this, and I will be his God and he will be My son.*
> **Revelation 21:6**

In that moment, the Lord gave me eyes to see Him for who He is and a heart to believe what He said. He has authority over me, everything I can see and can't see. And His desire for me was clear, His invitation sincere. I was less than a microscopic dot in the world, let alone the entire universe, and here He was, standing over all of it, inviting me to be His son.

Though a small city was often too much space to cross for my earthly dad, my heavenly Father bridged eternity through His Son, Jesus, for me. And that night, sitting alone in my bedroom as I spent most nights, He saved me.

The Lord has stripped away the loneliness and shame of my youth. Fast forward 25 years and I am faithfully married to the most remarkable woman and the dad not just to one son or two sons, but three incredible sons. I am surrounded by amazing friends, who are better men, Stronger Men, and am a part of a vibrant, Jesus-loving church doing all it can to help more people meet, love and follow Jesus. And, most precious of all, I am my Father's son.

Kyle, 42

REFLECT & DISCUSS

1. What is your biggest takeaway from this chapter?

_____

_____

_____

2. When did you "wake up" to the reality of God? What did that look like? Did you grow up with an awareness of His presence or did that come later in life?

_____

_____

_____

3. Why is it important that God chooses to reveal Himself as our Heavenly Father?

_____

_____

_____

4. What does "pretense" look like for you when interacting with God? What would it look like for you to get rid of pretense in your relationship with Him?

_____

_____

_____

5. What comes to mind when you reflect on the reality that God is near to you at every moment (His "immanence")? How have you experienced the nearness of God in your own life?

_____

_____

_____

6. Have you ever spoken out loud to God in private? Why or why not?

_____

_____

_____

7. What specific invitation do you sense God the Father extending to you as you read this chapter?

_____

_____

_____

TAKE ACTION

Set aside 30-60 minutes this week to spend talking to and listening to your Heavenly Father. Here are some helpful tips:

- Pick a day and time and put it in your calendar.
- Pick a private place where you won't be disturbed.
- **Speak out loud** when praying.
- Start with Scripture to prepare your heart and mind. _Not sure where to start? Some good go-to texts are the Psalms (Psalms 5, 8, 17, 18, 27, 42, 91, 103, 139, or 145)._
- Bring paper and a pen.
- Put in your calendar the next time that you'll spend time alone with your Father.

WEEK 8

GOOD FATHER, GOOD GIFTS

Which of you fathers, if your son asks for a fish, will give him a snake instead? Or if he asks for an egg, will give him a scorpion? If you then, though you are evil, know how to give good gifts to your children, how much more will your Father in Heaven give the Holy Spirit to those who ask Him!

LUKE 11:11-13

Stronger Men live in the blessing and confidence of their Good Father who gives good gifts to His children.

"The Lord's Prayer" is found in two places in the New Testament. In Matthew 6:9-13 and in Luke 11:1-4.

In Luke's account of the Lord's prayer, Jesus follows the teaching with a story and follow up instruction about the nature of prayer and how we are to view and approach God. He includes a "lesser-to-greater" analogy of comparing God first to a friend, then, with even greater emphasis ("how much more"), a good Father.

Here's what Luke writes:

> Then Jesus said to them, "Suppose you have a friend, and you go to him at midnight and say, 'Friend, lend me three loaves of bread; a friend of mine on a journey has come to me, and I have no food to offer him.' And suppose the one inside answers, 'Don't bother me. The door is already locked, and my children and I are in bed. I can't get up and give you anything.' I tell you, even though he will not get up and give you the bread because of friendship, yet because of your shameless audacity he will surely get up and give you as much as you need."

> "So I say to you: Ask and it will be given to you; seek and you will find; knock and the door will be opened to you. For everyone who asks receives; the one who seeks finds; and to the one who knocks, the door will be opened."

> "Which of you fathers, if your son asks for a fish, will give him a snake instead? Or if he asks for an egg, will give him a scorpion? If you then, though you are evil, know how to give good gifts to your children, how much more will your Father in Heaven give the Holy Spirit to those who ask Him!"

Do you see what Jesus is teaching here and what He intentionally presses home?

How are we to view God? How are we to approach God? How does God respond to our needs and our earnest requests?

Even a friend can be moved to respond to our boldness, persistence, or shameless audacity.

Think of who you would consider your closest friends. Who would you call late at night with a pressing need? Who would you risk bothering at an inconvenient time? Who would you call in a favor from?

In telling this story, Jesus is teaching His disciples that God, in one very real sense, is inviting us to "bother" Him!

Theologians call this "importunity." It's persistence even to the point of annoyance.

It's like that persistent neighbor kid who comes by your house selling cookies for their fundraiser. It's okay to admit that you're not always thrilled by the first request. Maybe the second request doesn't move you. But finally, you relent. "Fine. Good job being persistent. I'll take 10. Here you go."

If we're honest, we might even give in occasionally to a friend's incessant request, just to get them off our back! We're guys here, we can be honest. Ever said to yourself, "*Just say 'yes,' help him out, and be done with it. This is the fifth time he's asked you to help him move the piano, he's going to keep asking.*"

Jesus is saying, "Look, even a friend can be annoyed and bothered into meeting your repeated request. So, by all means, keep asking, keep seeking, keep knocking."

There's an aspect of prayer that has that element in it: Ask! Seek! Knock!

And yet this isn't anywhere near the fullness of what the Lord wants for us or offers to us. Seeing God as a friend who can be woken to help, aroused to action, may be a first step, but it's not the full picture.

God is so much more and so much better! He's not just a friend who can be bothered into blessing you.

He's a Father who LOVES to BLESS His children.

And He's available with unrestricted access, 24/7.

He draws near at the sound of your voice. He knows what you need. He's thought of everything in advance. He's providing for it all. He has wisdom and perspective beyond what you or I are capable of comprehending.

If you're a dad, even though you know you're not perfect, you still know how to give good gifts and meet the basic needs of your children when they ask. But Jesus doesn't pull any punches. He says plainly, "*If you then, **though you are evil**, know how to give good gifts to your children...*" Ouch! But it's true.

Then comes the punchline, "How much more will your Father in Heaven give the Holy Spirit to those who ask!"

Let those three words sink into your soul: How. Much. More.

There's truly no comparison. As I heard Louie Giglio say, God is not the reflection of your earthly father but the perfection of everything a good dad is and should be.

His love for you is perfect. His watchful care over you is unmatched.

He's not playing games with you or withholding blessings from you.

You're not a burden or a bother to Him. That's what the enemy wants you to think. But it's a lie.

You're God's boy.

He's waiting to pour out blessing on you and within you—most powerfully and specifically—His very presence, His own Holy Spirit.

He's ready to give you the greatest gift there is: Himself.

You have full access, full blessing. You can have full confidence, full peace, full assurance.

Think of how this truth could and should change your thinking and change your life?

From fear and anxiety to confidence and peace.

From angst and pressure to rest and relief.

From uncertainty and distance to security and assurance.

God is a good Father. And He loves to give good gifts to His kids.

When you think back over your childhood, what was a favorite gift you received for Christmas? Or one that stands out to you? Maybe it was from your dad or your mom or a family member. Or maybe, like one friend of mine, it came from a bunch of loving Christians at a local church who donated gifts to children in need. And this friend, who grew up homeless, remembers the joy and impact of receiving something new and needed at Christmas time from people he never met.

What gift comes to your mind?

What do you remember about it? What thoughts and feelings come to mind?

I remember the year my brothers and I got new skateboards. Or the year we got the original Nintendo. Mario Bros. and Duck Hunt, anyone?

I remember the GT Snow Racer sled I got one year. And a new Walkman cassette player. Don't know what this is? Ask your dad.

We always got something we wanted, and we always got things we needed.

Every year, we would get new Christmas pajamas and new thermal underwear.

It may sound so simple and silly, but as I look back and think about those simple, modest gifts, it brings tears to my eyes.

My good, earthly father, "though he was evil," did his best to bless his three boys.

My dad ran a grocery store in a town of 500 people and my mom was a teacher's aide helping kids learn to read and write at the local K-12 school. But they scraped together a warm, thoughtful, generous Christmas every year that felt like a bounty of blessing and grace.

My dad blessed us. And yet, as we grew, we knew it was simply what he and my mom could responsibly afford. It was the best they could do. It was awesome.

I've grown up and now have four children of my own. I now know, firsthand, the feeling of sitting in the seat of "dad," wanting to provide the best I can for my kids. Nothing beats the joy and excitement on their faces. And if you're like me, you always wish you could do so much more.

Friends, "how much more will your heavenly Father give (good gifts) the Holy Spirit, to those who ask Him!"

In 2016, Chris Tomlin released the song "Good, Good Father," written by Pat Barrett and Tony Brown, that quickly became a number one most-played song on radio stations across the country. The lyrics and music touched a nerve, the deep longing for the unmatched, undeniable love of God, that is hardwired to our souls. The searching is inescapable, regardless of our wild attempts to insulate, isolate, medicate, stuff down, toughen up, push through, ignore, deny, or pretend it's not there.

Men, this is good news. We can lay down the fear, the pride, the hurt, the tough exterior, the endless worldly pursuit, and the broken views of God.

And we can come under the waterfall of blessing, the endless grace, the unchanging love, the mind-blowing mercy, the perfect peace of our Good Father, who gives good gifts.

Stronger Men sit in this reality regularly and soak in His blessing and love.

I wonder what good gift He has for you and me today?

LET'S PRAY

Father, bless my brothers reading this today. Show them what You are truly like and remind them how available and accessible You are in this moment. Pour out Your Holy Spirit upon them, enabling them to know and receive Your love and Your good gifts and blessing. Fill them with strength and boldness and perseverance to keep asking, keep seeking, and keep knocking, all while knowing You're so much more than a bothered friend who will reluctantly give in. You're a good Father ready, willing, and able to bless them today. In Jesus' Name, amen.

FROM A STRONGER MAN

"If I have seen further, it is by standing on the shoulders of giants."
-Isaac Newton.

My dad's got strong shoulders—shoulders that have carried a lot over 30 years of pastoring churches, and I'm where I'm at today because I have the blessing of standing upon his faithfulness. My dad is a humble man. He'd be the first to admit that he was a flawed father, but he succeeded in some of the most important areas. He led me to Jesus, disciplined my sin, gave me a biblical foundation for my life, and let me know often that he loved me.

It was in my dad's arms as a young boy that, with tears, I placed my faith in Jesus. It was my dad who baptized me in the Wenatchee River. He would sit on the edge of my bed and pray with me every night before going to sleep—all the way until I left for college! I have many memories of my dad reading his well-worn Bible, the same one he opened as he officiated my wedding. These days, my dad gets to hold my children in his arms. He's reaping the benefits of long obedience in the same direction.

I honor my father—I have a great dad! And yet, we are both sons of a better Father. I have the blessing of being my dad's brother in Christ. One day we will stand before our Father as sons coming home. My dad will probably beat me there, but my eye is on that day. I look towards that reunion, that moment, with eager anticipation.

When I think of the spiritual legacy I want to leave behind, when I envision the man I want to be in 50 years, my dad's example looms large in my mind. He's been married to my mom for 37 years. He has four adult children who love Jesus passionately and have married incredible, godly spouses. We're all raising our kids to love and serve Jesus.

That's success. Faithfulness. Obedience. Legacy.

When I stand before my Father in Heaven, that's what I want to be true of me: "He followed Jesus faithfully. He loved his wife well. He showed his kids the better Father. He poured blessing into the lives of his grandkids. He lived with eternity in mind. He poured his life out in service to King Jesus."

And one day, I long to hear the words, "Well done, good and faithful servant. Welcome home, my son."

This is my prayer for you as well, my brother. May you live for that day.

AJ, 25

Like his father before him, my dad knew how to work hard. To this day, my dad can still outwork me, and he's in his 60s now. I've met few men in my life who have the dogged determination to see a job through to the end like my father.

The older I get, the more I come awake to the many blessings of growing up in his home. My father loved me like a son needs to be loved by their dad: as a small child he held me, and told me often that he loved me. As a boy, he played ball with me, read the Bible to me, and taught me how to work, and how to fish. As a young man, he challenged me, held me accountable, and disciplined me. And like my brother AJ wrote, for 18 years he sat on the edge of my bed every night that he was home and earnestly prayed for me, asking for the Lord's protection and for His blessing on my life. I thank God that His faithful prayers have been answered a thousand times over.

There's many things I could tell you about my dad if given the time, but if I had to tell you one thing, it would be this: **My father knew how to do the hard thing**. He knew how to carry weight. He consistently got the job done, whatever that "job" happened to be that day.

When things in life got tough, difficult, complex, downright gross, or exhausting, I'd watch my dad focus his gaze, set his jaw, suck in a breath of air through gritted teeth and wade into whatever situation was presenting itself—whether dealing with a poop-stained diaper blowout from a sick kid, setting a glue lam beam with only his own shoulders and his nail gun, or getting ready to sit down at the church office for a pastoral intervention with someone. I saw my dad's heart revealed in situations no one else would want to find themselves in, and yet, where no one else's presence would have succeed.

But what I appreciate most about my dad is that he completed the most important job that he was given: the job of leading his family in such a way that his children would grow up to love their heavenly Father.

My dad wasn't a perfect father; I wasn't a perfect son, and I'm not a perfect husband and father to my wife and two little boys today. Far from it.

But the point is this: my father led his family to Jesus.

And though I struggle with uneven steps to follow in my dad's footprints, I am endeavoring with all I am to lead my family to follow after the King like he did.

When things in my own life, family, and ministry get tough, difficult, complex, downright gross or exhausting, I remember the example of my earthly father, who taught me to focus my gaze on my heavenly Father, set my jaw, suck in a breath of air through gritted teeth, wade in, and get the job done.

May God give me the grace to faithfully do my job as my father has done his.

Adam, 29

REFLECT & DISCUSS

1. What is your biggest takeaway from this chapter?

_____

_____

_____

2. What is one gift that you received in the past that you remember now? Why do you remember it?

_____

_____

_____

3. How would your life be different if you remembered more often that you have 24/7 access to your requests being seen and heard by your heavenly Father?

_____

_____

_____

4. Do you struggle to believe that God wants to bless you? Why or why not?

_____

_____

_____

5. God is a better Father than any earthly father. In what ways have you experienced failures or mistakes, your own or your dad's, and in what ways has God proven Himself to be a better, perfect Father? Share any examples that come to mind.

_____

_____

_____

6. What good gifts has God given you?

_____

_____

_____

7. Think of the last time you took a moment to sincerely thank God for His gifts. Has He been good to you since that time?

_____

_____

_____

TAKE ACTION

- Make a plan to give your wife and each of your kids the "gift" of intentional 1-on-1 time over the next few weeks and/or month. What would they want to do? What would be a special afternoon or evening in their eyes? What activities would you do? What places would you go? What would you talk about?

- If you don't have kids or are unmarried, how could you give the gift of your intentional time and attention to someone you're close to in your life that would be blessed by it? (e.g. wife, parents, siblings)

WEEK 9

LOVING DISCIPLINE
FROM A FAITHFUL FATHER

Endure hardship as discipline; God is treating you as His children. For what children are not disciplined by their father? If you are not disciplined—and everyone undergoes discipline—then you are not legitimate, not true sons and daughters at all. Moreover, we have all had human fathers who disciplined us and we respected them for it. How much more should we submit to the Father of spirits and live! They disciplined us for a little while as they thought best; but **GOD DISCIPLINES US FOR OUR GOOD,** in order that we may share in His holiness. No discipline seems pleasant at the time, but painful. Later on, however, it produces a harvest of righteousness and peace for those who have been trained by it.

HEBREWS 12:7-11

I wish I could see a thought bubble appear over your head when you first think about the word "discipline."

I'm going to go out on a limb and guess that it wouldn't be an expression of joy and excitement.

I'm picturing something along the lines of "ugh" or "dang" or any one of the painful face emojis we use in text messages.

I'm also willing to guess that your thoughts and feelings about discipline have changed or will change as you grow. I hope so.

It used to be only a negative word or concept to me, but then I realized just how important and necessary it is to become a more disciplined person and how essential discipline is toward growth, strength, and success in anything and everything in our lives.

My experiences in sports taught me the power and impact of discipline. If you want to make a high percentage of your free throws or 3-pointers, you've got to exercise high levels of discipline for your mind and body to be conformed to the necessary action of accurately shooting a basketball.

Watching others become proficient in a musical instrument, physically fit, or competent in any skill, you see the fruit and reward of discipline on display.

The same is true of our character, our spiritual maturity, our faithfulness as lovers of our wives and children, our healthy contributions in any relationship or endeavor, and our overall strength as men.

The writer of Hebrews tells us, "*No discipline seems pleasant at the time, but painful. Later on, however, it produces a harvest of righteousness and peace for those who have been trained by it.*"

HARSH FATHERS

Some men had bad examples and experiences with the harsh discipline of a father. Over the years, I've heard horrific stories of angry, out-of-control dads reigning down terror, pain, physical abuse, and verbal and emotional destruction on helpless sons. Perhaps this is what they also received from their fathers. Regardless of what factors contributed to this experience of harsh and unrighteous discipline, let this be clear: it was and is totally evil, inexcusably harmful, and simultaneously angers and breaks the heart of God the Father in the moment it is occurring.

If that's ever been your story, I'm truly sorry and I want you to know that kind of "discipline" is wicked abuse, plain and simple, and has no place in the homes of Stronger Men.

Fathers, do not provoke your children to anger. **Ephesians 6:4**

Fathers, do not embitter your children, or they will become discouraged. **Colossians 3:21**

There is no fear in love. But perfect love drives out fear, because fear has to do with punishment. The one who fears is not made perfect in love. **1 John 4:18**

But now you must also rid yourselves of all such things as these: anger, rage, malice, slander, and filthy language from your lips. **Colossians 3:8**

THE NEED FOR FORGIVENESS

If that has been any part of your story, as hard as it may be to hear, you will need to grapple with the supernatural work of forgiveness in order to be free from the generational curse brought on by your father's anger and abuse.

The good news is you have a loving Father in Heaven who can heal you and empower you to release the judgment toward wrongs done to you and trust that God, as a perfect Judge in the higher court of Heaven, knows how to perfectly and justly deal with the sins of a father. They will either be punished in eternal wrath and righteous judgment in Hell, or were already punished in the crucified body of Jesus Christ on the cross, as He absorbed the wrath of God against sinners.

Jesus Christ is able to forgive those who repent.

Furthermore, says the Lord, "Vengeance is mine, I will repay." We cannot improve upon God's judgment or justice, we can only harm ourselves by giving in to the demonic stronghold of bitterness and unforgiveness.

The key to extending forgiveness to others is first receiving forgiveness for our own sins. No man heals who stays in the place of victimhood and justifies or excuses his own sin because of what was done to him. Only through realizing one's own sin and sinful responses, and receiving the grace of Jesus, can a man be filled with the strength and ability to extend forgiveness to those who've wronged him.

This does not mean you "deserved" what happened to you. That's not what I'm saying nor what the Bible teaches. As children, we do not deserve abuse. We don't deserve to be treated harshly in a vulnerable station. But as sinners ourselves, we must recognize as we grow up, we too are deserving of the wrath of God and in need of forgiveness.

Even if your father is no longer alive, or unable or unwilling to repent, you can still release the poison of unforgiveness and allow God to be Judge and walk in the freedom of releasing the burden of another man's debt.

NEGLECTFUL FATHERS

Other men have experienced dads who were totally absent or completely checked out and, therefore, had no discipline brought to their attitudes or actions. Though a different form, this neglect is also extremely harmful and unloving.

Absent and passive forms of discipline are far too prevalent in our day of soft and weak men and fathers. If you fail to properly discipline your son, you are knowingly or unknowingly hating your son, and creating a future burden on anyone who ends up in relationship with him.

Women, children, society, and future sons all suer from the lack of true discipline from godly fathers.

The lack of discipline wreaks all kinds of havoc on the character formation of young men. Attitudes of entitlement, low self-respect, lack of confidence, depression, anxiety, self-pity, self-doubt, lack of security, and emotional bankruptcy, all result from the absence of proper loving discipline.

If this has been part of your story, you too will have to walk the road of freedom through forgiveness and healing that comes from the perfect love of our heavenly Father.

Both abusive or absent forms of discipline are expressions of hate and evil toward sons.

FAITHFUL FATHERS

Thankfully, through God's grace, some men had good examples and experiences with the discipline of their fathers and they should respect, honor, and thank them for the blessing of loving discipline.

The generational blessing that comes from a father who models his discipline after the principles and character of God the Father is a powerful blessing indeed. The foundation that tough and tender love and discipline provides is like an inheritance that flows to a son. That son is given a great opportunity to stand on faithful shoulders and impact his own generation with fewer hurts and hurdles to overcome in the journey of faith and future fatherhood.

But even faithful fathers don't ultimately provide the fullness of blessing that God designed. They are like springboards launching us in the direction of our heavenly Father or windows through which we can see and subsequently pursue the glory of our perfect Father.

THE PERFECT FATHER

God the Father does not "punish" His sons, deal with them harshly, or neglect them, but rather disciplines them in love. His discipline is for their good, as a means of instructing and molding them into strong, confident, responsible, capable men of faithful character, who know they have been perfectly loved.

Likewise, Stronger Men learn to discipline their own children in a self-controlled, purposeful, redemptive, and loving way.

THE DANGER OF ALL DISCIPLINE

Even when good discipline is being applied to a son, it's a vulnerable moment of temptation.

Proverbs tells us, "*My son, do not despise the Lord's discipline and do not resent His rebuke, because the Lord disciplines those He loves, as a father the son he delights in*" (**Proverbs 3:11-12**).

All of us have a default position of bucking discipline. It's the result of our sinful and prideful condition.

Therefore, when it comes to the loving discipline of our earthly fathers or the perfect discipline of our heavenly Father, sons young and old must have a right understanding of discipline and a right response to discipline.

Consider 8 Principles of Discipline from Hebrews 12:7-11:

#1 For a stronger man, all hardship that comes into his life is a form of redemptive, productive discipline (v. 7)

Stronger Men know that God is sovereign over everything that comes into their lives and everything will be turned for good in the life of a man who trusts in God. "*And we know that in all things God works for*

115

the good of those who love Him, who have been called according to His purpose" (**Romans 8:28**). This is not a cheap promise but a deep and profound reality that must get infused into the bones of any man who desires to be used greatly by God. The Greek word for "discipline" in this passage is the word 'paideia.' It's a powerful word with no precise English equivalent. It is holistic training and instruction aimed at increased virtue and total soul formation.

#2 Hardship requires endurance (v. 7)

Here we are back to the call to be soldiers. "*You then, my SON, be strong in the grace that is in Christ Jesus...and endure hardship like a good SOLDIER of Christ Jesus*" (**2 Timothy 2:1,3**). "Endure hardship as discipline." Discipline is not harsh, but it is hard. And hard means hard. Stronger Men endure hardship and get better for it.

#3 Discipline from the Father is a sign of our legitimacy as sons (v. 8)

Sons need discipline and every good father disciplines his son. God is the best Father. He doesn't abandon us in discipline. Rather, He proves the genuineness of our adoption as His legitimate sons through discipline. He is treating us as His precious children. Stronger Men are true sons of the Father.

#4 Good discipline results in respect, honor, and gratitude (v. 9)

Discipline is best seen and understood in hindsight. The reward is a lag measurement. It comes later, as a result of the discipline. Stronger Men know the value of discipline and are grateful where applicable to their earthly dads and ultimately to the Lord who deserves all respect.

#5 Discipline requires submission (v. 9)

This is why it's a challenge for most men. Men don't naturally submit easily. But Stronger Men know the secret to life is found in submission to God the Father. Resistance is futile and foolish. Surrender brings victory. The sooner we give in, the sooner we grow up.

#6 Discipline is redemptive and purposeful, producing strong moral character (v. 10)

Discipline is redemptive, not punitive. It's purposeful, not pointless. God disciplines us for our good, that we may share in His holiness. Discipline from God purifies, forges, forms, and sets apart. Stronger Men see the gift and growth that come wrapped in the pain of discipline. A man who has been disciplined deeply walks with the aroma of holiness. He's been forged in the fire, and he's emerged battle ready.

#7 Discipline hurts (v. 11)

It's okay to admit it. Stronger Men don't ignore or deny pain. They face it honestly, trust the Father, and endure. "*No discipline seems pleasant at the time, but painful.*" Therefore, we tread lightly with a brother who is in the midst of it. It hurts. At the time, it sucks. Don't be flippant. It hurts, and by God's grace, this too shall pass. But that's not always the best thing to hear at the time. Stronger Men are wise, careful, and shrewd with their words during someone else's time of discipline.

#8 We have to rightly respond to discipline to reap its rewards (v. 11)

In our lives as men, when a test comes, if you don't pass it, you just get to take it again. "*Discipline produces a harvest of peace and righteousness to those who have been trained by it.*" We must be teachable, trainable, and humble learners. Harvest comes after hard work. As a result, the fruit of discipline rightly responded to is especially sweet. It has a way of subduing our unbridled passions and bringing peace, rest, and righteousness to the soul. In times of discipline, slow down. Study hard, think deeply, and respond humbly. When you pass the test, you'll reap the rewards, and you'll experience the love of the Father in greater ways than ever before.

A FINAL THOUGHT

When it comes to hardship, pain, and discipline, our perspective is vital, our posture is key, our faith is essential, and our Father is faithful.

LET'S PRAY

Father, help us as men submit to You and live. Help us trust Your perfect and faithful discipline in our lives. Comfort any man reading this in the throws of hardship. Instruct every man in the wisdom of humility. Thank You for treating us as true sons and not neglecting us or being harsh with us but perfectly training us and molding us to be effective sons whom You can trust with greater responsibility and opportunity to impact others. Bring us through each season of discipline refined, stronger, and closer to You than ever before. In Jesus' Name, amen.

FROM A STRONGER MAN

When I was 10 years old my life was shattered after a series of poor decisions and addiction that led to my mom and dad getting divorced. Times were hard. Through all the despair, chaos, confusion, and hopelessness, my dad stepped up and provided for my two younger brothers and me. He pulled extra shifts, built a house while we lived in a trailer, and even pawned his wedding ring to buy groceries. My parents had split custody, so we grew up with two bedrooms, two Christmases, two bikes; the list goes on. Anyone out there who thinks it's cool to have two of everything, I assure you, it is not.

My dad raised us in a way that made it crystal clear that decisions have consequences, both good and bad, and those consequences do not just impact you. Dad's examples in his actions also taught me to always be the best version of myself, always assume the responsibility to help others, and always do more than what is expected. Even with the incredible example my dad set for us and the foundation he built, Jesus was not part of it. Looking back, Dad's ethics were aligned with a Biblical worldview, but without the acknowledgment these ethics were built on the foundation of God's Word. We were simply living out an earthly worldview. I thought as long as I lived up to my earthly father's standards, I would be considered a good person.

After 9/11 I graduated high school and despite being accepted into the prestigious Washington State University, I enlisted in the Marine Corps. **Some say you find Jesus in dark places. Well, I found Jesus at bootcamp. He was the only nice guy around and I preferred hanging out with him at church, for an hour, on Sunday instead of a drill instructor!** At the time, I was the only Christian in my immediate family. A year or so later, I married a godly woman and we knew it was our duty to lead our future children, the next Lewis generation, to know Christ. What I had not considered yet was my duty to lead the generation before me.

In 2007, I got out of the Marine Corps. That same year, after 32 years of serving the City of Seattle as a career detective, hunting down serial bank robbers, rapists, child predators, and murderers, my dad retired. As he removed his badge, Dad pinned on my badge as I embarked on my career in law enforcement. I spent 11 years working on the west side of Washington State and through God's incredible plan, I moved to an agency in North Central Washington. Through this leap of faith, the Lord paved the way for me to reprioritize my marriage and my relationship with my kids. Ironically, as I moved further away from my dad, we became closer.

When my family and I started attending Grace City Church, it became clear to me that my profession was to protect people from evil, but my mission from God was to help lead people away from it. Regardless of what they may tell you, no LEO, Chief, Sheri, or politician in this country has the ability to rid their community of evil. We can do our best to suppress it, but only Jesus can eradicate it.

Over the next few years, Dad would visit and I'd invite him to church but he would find an excuse to decline the offer. I was frustrated because I knew Dad had spent a lifetime saving others but had not yet been saved himself. This was constantly on my heart and I invited him to the Stronger Man Conference in 2021 and 2022. The first year was a blast. The second was a miracle.

On the first night of the "Forged" conference, Pastor Josh gave an ultimatum. You are either on God's side or Satan's. "YOUR MOVE." I sat there silently praying for my dad. At that moment, my dad and my brother stood up, turned their backs to Satan, and walked into the loving arms of their Savior. Finally, after my dad spent a lifetime saving others, he had been saved by Jesus Christ. My little brother, his third son, followed his lead to the altar.

A few months later, Pastor Josh and I baptized my dad. As he rose from the water and hugged me, I acknowledged that this wasn't a hug from a father to a son. I was embracing a brother in Christ and we will spend eternity together with our Father.

Throughout my military and law enforcement career, I have had a front-row seat to what I consider a 21-year crash course on leadership. Leadership is commonly thought of as the ability to influence those under one's authority or control. However, I have learned not to dismiss our ability and responsibility to lead up. The story of my dad's salvation is a miraculous example of how we as sons can lead up, so those before us may meet, love, and follow Jesus.

Stay bold. Stay persistent. Stay strong.

Brian, 38

REFLECT & DISCUSS

1. What is your biggest takeaway from this chapter?

_____

_____

_____

2. Would you say you have a generally positive view of discipline? Why or why not?

_____

_____

_____

3. Think about what kind of father you had in regards to discipline and correction. Was he a harsh father, a neglectful father, or a faithful father? What truth from the chapter speaks directly to what you experienced from your father?

_____

_____

_____

4. "Discipline hurts" (Hebrews 12:11). Describe a time where you felt the painful, yet ultimately necessary and helpful, discipline of God in your life. What good did God bring about in your life as a result of that time of discipline?

_____

_____

_____

5. In what way do you need to grow in order to embrace the reality that God allows hardship into your life (Hebrews 7) in order to form you and mold you into the man He wants you to be?

_____

_____

_____

6. Where do you want/need God to change/discipline you? What prayer do you need to pray?

_____

_____

_____

7. What would it look like for you to embrace the discipline of your Heavenly Father?

_____

_____

_____

TAKE ACTION

- Make a list of 10 difficult things you have endured in your life. For each of the 10 items, write down how God has used it, is using it currently, or could use it to mold you and transform you into a Stronger Man.

- Share it with another Stronger Man *this week*.

121

WEEK 10

THREE ATTRIBUTES OF LOVING FATHERS

For you know that we dealt with each of you as a father deals with his own children, ENCOURAGING, COMFORTING AND URGING YOU TO LIVE LIVES WORTHY OF GOD, who calls you into His Kingdom and glory.

1 THESSALONIANS 2:11-12

God puts strong fathers or stronger men who are like spiritual fathers in men's lives for their good.

These kinds of men bless us and equip us through their example and through their encouraging, comforting, and urging words. They compel us to live into the great call of God upon our lives.

To the degree that men walk in humble integrity before God, other men's lives are enriched by their efforts and input.

Think for a moment; who has been most significant to you in the development of your faith? Which men has God used in your life to help you grow and mature the most?

Stop and think about words they said, questions they asked, and things they did to positively impact you.

In these few short verses in 1 Thessalonians, a little New Testament letter to a thriving little church, we find some of the most helpful instruction about the nature of good fathering and spiritual leadership in the entire New Testament.

I love the letter of 1 Thessalonians. It's one of my favorite books. They were like the little church that could.

The world was going crazy and they found themselves in a very antagonistic cultural environment. In addition, false teachers and naysayers were spreading rumors concerning the second coming of Christ. Some were even saying it had already happened and they had missed it.

Paul wrote to assure them and instruct them about these things and also to encourage them for the genuineness of their faith, hope, and love.

In the midst of persecution and cultural chaos, their faith was thriving.

They were a model of faith and good works, of love and sincere labor, and of hope and endurance.

Listen to how Paul describes them in the first chapter of his first letter to them:

> *For we know, brothers and sisters loved by God, that He has chosen you, because our gospel came to you not simply with words but also with power, with the Holy Spirit and deep conviction. You know how we lived among you for your sake. You became imitators of us and of the Lord, for you welcomed the message in the midst of severe suffering with the joy given by the Holy Spirit. And so you became a model to all the believers in Macedonia and Achaia. The Lord's message rang out from you not only in*

Macedonia and Achaia—your faith in God has become known everywhere. Therefore we do not need to say anything about it, for they themselves report what kind of reception you gave us. They tell how you turned to God from idols to serve the living and true God, and to wait for His Son from Heaven, whom He raised from the dead—Jesus, who rescues us from the coming wrath.
1 Thessalonians 1:4-10

And Paul loved them like his spiritual children. He called them his "glory and joy."

In the second chapter, he tells them that his paradigm for ministry to them was to emulate the way a good father deals with his children.

*For you know that we dealt with each of you **as a father deals with his own children, <u>encouraging</u>, <u>comforting</u> and <u>urging</u>** you to live lives worthy of God, who calls you into His Kingdom and glory.*
1 Thessalonians 2:11-12

The first time I read that verse as a young father, I knew I had stumbled across a simple, clear, divinely inspired mission statement and aim for my own responsibility and calling as a dad (and also as a pastor).

A good, loving dad deals with his children in three essential ways, for which Paul uses three distinct Greek words:

- Encouraging/Exhorting—'Parakaleo'
- Comforting/Consoling—'Paramytheomai'
- Urging/Charging/Imploring—'Martyromai'

What does it look, sound, and feel like to be encouraged and exhorted? To encourage and exhort?

What does it look, sound, and feel like to be comforted? To comfort?

What does it look, sound, and feel like to be urged to live a life worthy of God who calls you into His Kingdom and glory? To do that for others?

Answer those questions and you're well on your way toward being a loving, exemplary Christian father—a strong spiritual leader and builder of men.

Those three actions—encouraging, comforting, and urging—and their resulting influence are a road map for godly, spiritual leadership and loving, spiritual authority.

Let's briefly take a closer look at some definitions based on the biblical use of these three words.

1. 'Parakaleo'—translated "encouraging," "exhorted"

➡ to call to one's side, call for, summon

➡ to address, speak to, (call to, call upon), which may be done in the way of exhortation, entreaty, comfort, instruction, etc.

2. 'Paramytheomai' - translated "comforting"

➡ to speak to, address one, whether by way of admonition and incentive, or to calm and console

➡ to encourage, console

➡ As in John 11, comforting Mary and Martha at the loss of their brother, Lazarus. Comforting and consoling the disheartened.

3. 'Martyromai' - translated "urging," "imploring"

➡ to cite a witness, bring forward a witness, call to witness

➡ to arm by appeal to God, to declare solemnly, protest

➡ to conjure, beseech as in God's Name, exhort solemnly

STRONGER DADS
ENCOURAGE & EXHORT

When you consider that one of the Greek words for the "Holy Spirit" is 'paraklētos' or 'Paraclete,' which means "one who comes alongside" and is often translated "Helper," you can see the related nature of the word Paul uses for "encouraging" in 1 Thessalonians 2:11-12.

Just as the Holy Spirit comes alongside us as followers of Jesus, to help us and comfort us and counsel us, so too fathers come alongside and call their sons and daughters to watch, listen, and learn from them.

A father is a helper, a teacher, an encourager, an exhorter.

Dads look their kids in their eyes, with a loving hand on their shoulder, and use their words to carefully instruct, encourage, and exhort their children in the ways of God.

Kids should get a lot of face time, eye contact, and verbal encouragement from their dads.

It is dads who call out for their children to "come here" in order to be instructed and encouraged, in a loving and empowering way.

Notice that the sense in which this is calling for is more positive than corrective. It's not that we don't correct our sons, we most certainly do. But they ought to hear more encouragement and positive instruction from us than negative or corrective. Too many men have testimonies of only hearing "what they did wrong" from their dad.

Empowering dads look for ways and opportunities to tell their children *well done*, *great job*, and *attaboy*. Dads have incredible power to use their words to build up or tear down. Our aim should be to instill courage and confidence, not to merely critique performance and increase demands.

As loving fathers, we must use our words to express our love to and for our kids. They should regularly hear us say, "I love you," no matter how unnatural or awkward that feels or sounds coming out of our mouths.

Whether you ever heard your dad say it or not, your heavenly Father, and good spiritual fathers, say it often with sincerity.

Some men have never heard those kinds of words spoken over them, and that is a shame. I pray that even as you read this chapter, or these very words, you can hear the Father saying to you, "*I love you, son! Come here, listen close, I love you, I'm for you...keep going, you're doing good, I'm here, I'm with you. Watch out for those potholes. Stay away from the cliffs. Stay on your guard. But keep going. Stay in the fight. Trust Me and stick close. You got this. I saw the way you ran hard yesterday, I'm proud of you. Keep it up! Stay the course!*"

Can you hear Him?

The Father's heart and aim is to build us up!

I love the word "encouragement." Encouragement is not a weak word, though we sometimes think of it in those terms. It literally means to "put courage in."

A vital way that we become Stronger Men, grow as Stronger Men, and build up other Stronger Men is through the power of encouragement. Not sappy sentimental encouragement but true, biblical, Spirit-born, fist tap to the chest, eye-to-eye, hand-on-shoulder, man-to-man "putting courage in" kind of encouragement.

The ministry of biblical encouragement is a critical ingredient to a generation-shaping movement of godly men and manhood.

And it's a key to all godly fatherhood. A son should receive a barrage of encouragement from his dad. And men should give and receive a barrage of encouragement to each other.

STRONGER DADS
COMFORT

Comfort is another form of fatherly love in action. This is NOT just the role or responsibility of moms.

A loving father should notice and discern when his sons and daughters are discouraged, disheartened, or defeated—when they are sad or hurting.

This means a dad is to be emotionally aware and in tune with the hearts and countenances of his kids. Your EQ is actually more important than your IQ when it comes to fathering.

We all experience low points as we grow up. Dads are made for low points. The power of a father's comforting presence, consoling words, and heartfelt prayers build unbreakable bonds.

A father's primary aim is to be the blessing of loving presence, not the burden of heavy pressure.

Whenever our sons experience loss, death, or grief, we as dads must step into those moments of pain. This is also true if you're a young man learning to come alongside your friends or your siblings. You can begin to practice strong, loving, spiritual leadership even now.

The shortest verse in the Bible, "Jesus wept," is also one of the most profound. Jesus entered into grief with Mary and Martha at the death of their brother, Lazarus, even though He was about to raise him from the dead! Jesus was able to express compassion and comfort, to step into moments of deep emotion and pain, and connect and come alongside those who were hurting.

Stronger Men can do the same. The ability to grieve and mourn and comfort others in their hurt is the mark of a Stronger Man, not a weaker man. We are thick-skinned leaders, and tender-hearted lovers.

STRONGER DADS
URGE & IMPLORE

A Stronger Man knows when to bring seriousness and when to bring solemness into the fathering or leadership relationship. We are playing for keeps. The bullets are real. Young and immature men are given to foolishness and temptation.

Therefore, it is a dad's job to impress upon his son the weight of eternal reality and to urge him to live a life worthy of the call of God. God, Himself, is ultimately the One calling our sons and daughters to live for His glory and His Kingdom.

Our sons should see, hear, and feel a passion in our hearts to leverage our lives for Jesus. We get one shot. We run one lap. We face a real enemy. Sin is constantly lurking.

Being an encouraging and comforting dad does not mean 24/7 "light-hearted-buddy-buddy-fun-and-games-goofy-silly-guy." There's a time to be silly and a time to be serious.

Dads must know when and how to implore their sons to a life of holy and serious pursuit of God and His Kingdom. We can't baby our boys. We must call them to maturity, call them to greatness, call them to godliness, call them to greater depth, and call them to spiritual vigilance and urgency.

They are being loved, built up, encouraged, and comforted as part of their formation and training to become men who make great spiritual battle and impact with their lives.

The things of God must grip the hearts of our sons and the best way for that to happen is if the things of God grip our hearts.

When our sons see and hear a serious pursuit of God in our lives, and have an encouraging relationship with us, it brings a convergence of the words, actions, and passions of a stronger dad that creates an upward draft of spiritual momentum that pulls our sons and daughters up into the call of God upon their lives.

This is the aim of fatherhood and spiritual leadership in the lives of sons and men.

LET'S PRAY

Father, I thank You for this son, this brother, this father, this man reading this. Would You build him up today. Would You speak a word of encouragement, comfort, or urging that he needs to hear today. Wherever he is in his life journey, and his relationship with You, would You call him close, look him in the eye, place Your hand upon his shoulder and tell him that You love him, that You're proud of him, that You are with him and available to help him become the man, the son, the father, the leader, the lover that You're calling him to be. Strengthen him today and use him today and in the days to come for Your Kingdom and Your glory. In Jesus' Name, amen.

Verses To Reflect On

*Therefore, I **urge** you, brothers and sisters, in view of God's mercy, to offer your bodies as a living sacrifice, holy and pleasing to God—this is your true and proper worship.* **Romans 12:1**

*I **urge** you, brothers and sisters, to watch out for those who cause divisions and put obstacles in your way that are contrary to the teaching you have learned. Keep away from them.* **Romans 16:17**

*We are therefore Christ's ambassadors, as though God were making His appeal through us. We **implore** you on Christ's behalf: Be reconciled to God.* **2 Corinthians 5:20**

*As for other matters, brothers and sisters, we **instructed** you how to live in order to please God, as in fact you are living. Now we ask you and **urge** you in the Lord Jesus to do this more and more.* **1 Thessalonians 4:1**

*Therefore **encourage** one another and **build each other up**, just as in fact you are doing.* **1 Thessalonians 5:11**

*But **encourage** one another daily, as long as it is called "Today," so that none of you may be hardened by sin's deceitfulness.* **Hebrews 3:13**

FROM A STRONGER MAN

With nervous determination, I lock eyes with the tall boy on the pitcher's mound. Now he steps to throw. I resolutely raise the bat off my shoulder. The ball flies at an impressive speed for 11-year-old little league. I swing, tracking to contact. A faint, yet undeniable sound, somewhere between clink and ting on the auditory gauge. I scan the horizon. No ball. Disappointment. A burst of yelling from the bleachers. I look down. There's the ball, about ten inches from my feet, in the dirt, and in play. The drama of the moment has cascaded into the anticlimax of a swinging bunt. With slight panic, my feet digging, and my arms pumping, I flail to first with all the speed and athleticism that a lanky 5th grade boy can conjure from the depths of his will—which is to say, high marks for theatrics, no marks for speed. I lurch and stretch my right leg forward, straining for the base. Across the infield, functionally miles away, the play is called by a 14-year-old umpire in baggy jeans and a blue polo —a symbol of laser accuracy and low self esteem, likely acquired from the verbal assaults of crazed moms. He utters with roughly the same decibel impact as the sound of my bat moments ago gingerly kissing the top of the baseball, which now rests nestled in the first baseman's glove. But it is loud enough. Safe. I keep my cool, but if my inner feeling of triumph were to manifest to this meager crowd, they would be tempted to believe I had just won the World Series with a walk off grand slam.

That's actually a story about my dad. No, he wasn't the 11-year-old boy who made it safely to first. That was, in fact, me. But he was the one who—when other dads may not have cared, or may not have tried, or may have even been embarrassed of his son's apparent inability to hit a baseball, or a beach ball for that matter—was the kind of dad who diligently taught me how to hit a baseball at a point in my boyhood when I was showing very little natural ability to do so. I was beginning to think I should quit playing, but my dad would not let me quit. Instead, he coached me, threw batting practice to me on Saturdays, and even borrowed an obscure VHS tape called "Dusty Baker Teaches Hitting." He popped it in, moved the living room furniture, brought me my bat, and let me swing away in front of the TV. When I beat that throw to first off of my swinging bunt, it was the first time I had made it to first all season. A minuscule victory in the hindsight of life, but a mountain of a memory in my imagination. A parable of the kind of man my dad is—one who, out of love, is masterfully intentional with his words and actions, to everyone, and especially to his own family.

"Intentional" is Dad's favorite word. For him, it captures the quality of what relationships should be for Christians. It describes God's action toward us. The Father wisely plans, the Son sacrificially accomplishes, the Spirit graciously applies salvation to us. Our redemption

is one hundred percent the result of God's intention. He initiates. He works. He loves. He draws us to Himself. Intentionality has permeated Dad's relationship with the Lord in response to His grace, as well as his love for others.

Over the years, some have thought of my dad as intense. One can quickly notice the relatedness of the word "intentional" to the word "intense." He has, in fact, been christened by his brothers in ministry with the nickname, "The General." I say that Dad is intense for all the right reasons, in exactly the way a man ought to be intense. Passive men are the Devil's pawns. My dad is no passive man. He is a passionate man. A man of deep affections. A man of great action. All of it borne from, and aimed toward, love for God, and love for people.

Growing up, I watched him dedicate himself to the Word of God with a blistering work ethic as a pastor. He toiled in the text, and through intense discipline and dependence on the Holy Spirit, faithfully taught the Bible from the deep conviction that people need the words of life. He built the culture of our home on the same foundation, teaching us Scripture, and showing us how to worship God by doing it himself.

And there was always joy. Some dads raise the stress level in their homes. My dad raised the happiness level. We laughed long, we worked hard, we played freely. Just as you could never accuse my dad of being passive, so you could never accuse him of being un-fun.

And through all of it, Dad was intentional, teaching me and my sisters that the chief end of man is to glorify God and enjoy Him forever. I can't remember ever truly doubting this God-centered vision for life, because Dad's integrity, *precisely as my dad*, proved to me that being a man formed by the glory of God is actually possible.

My dad's intentionality has borne the fruit of four decades of glorious marriage to my mom, a marriage that authentically displays Christ's love for the Church. His intentionality has resulted in all three of his now adult children faithfully following Jesus, with Christ-centered marriages of their own, raising children of their own to know the Lord. And his intentionality has impacted a literal multitude of students, men, and families.

As I lead my family, and obey God's call, Dad's favorite word increasingly grows in importance to me. Intentional is truly an encapsulating attribute of how a Stronger Man lives.

I thank my heavenly Father for giving me the kind of earthly father about whom I have always been proud to say, "I am the son of Kent McMullen."

Kyle, 34

REFLECT & DISCUSS

1. What is your biggest takeaway from this chapter? What stood out to you as you read?

_____

_____

_____

2. Who comes to your mind as a positive example of a man in your life who has encouraged, comforted, and urged you to live for God? How did he demonstrate these attributes?

_____

_____

_____

3. How did your dad do with giving and receiving comfort? How did he handle the emotions or experiences of grief, loss, sadness?

_____

_____

_____

4. How have you encountered grief, loss, and sadness in your life? How do you do with expressing and processing these emotions and giving and receiving comfort? What would it look like for you to grow and get "stronger" in this area?

_____

_____

_____

5. On a scale of 1-10, how comfortable are you having serious, significant conversations about spiritual things with your sons/daughters or other people? What would it take to grow in your ability to converse and become someone who can urge others biblically toward God's call on their life?

_____

_____

_____

6. What would it look like for you to "come alongside" your sons and/or other men in your life? In whose life could you be this kind of empowering influence in their life?

_____

_____

_____

7. What's one thing you could do this week to practice these three attributes (encourage, comfort, urge)?

_____

_____

_____

TAKE ACTION

Look for opportunities to follow through on your answer from question 7 above. Make note of the situation, how it went, what the fruit/result was, and anything you thought and felt in the process.

WEEK 11

LISTEN, MY SON, TO YOUR FATHER'S INSTRUCTION

MY SON, DO NOT FORGET MY TEACHING, BUT KEEP MY COMMANDS IN YOUR HEART, for they will prolong your life many years and bring you peace and prosperity. Let love and faithfulness never leave you; bind them around your neck, write them on the tablet of your heart. Then you will win favor and a good name in the sight of God and man. Trust in the Lord with all your heart and lean not on your own understanding; in all your ways submit to Him, and He will make your paths straight. Do not be wise in your own eyes; fear the Lord and shun evil.

PROVERBS 3:1-7

Stronger men learn to listen.

Admittedly, this has been an area of needed correction and instruction for most of my life. It was painfully obvious in my younger years. I was a ferocious talker. I still can be when I'm not careful. But, by God's grace, through intentional effort and the help of those who love me enough to call me out, I've become a much better listener and am much more self-aware and self-controlled in the use of my tongue and my ears.

One of my favorite teachers and coaches growing up was a very rough and colorful character. Everyone knew when Mr. Hunter, aka "Woody," was in the gym or at the game. He wasn't always the best example in his speech—that's an understatement—but he was a memorable character. If you knew "Woody," you either rolled your eyes and made a cringing expression, or you smiled and chuckled and got a kick out of his verbal rampages.

Although he was rough and abrasive and, at times, rude and crass, somehow he also managed to come across funny and lovable all rolled into one. He was an amazing storyteller and he actually had a tender heart tucked underneath the rough exterior.

And in a way, he was actually just what I needed.

He often told me, in his gravelly voice, "James, son, your mouth runs like a broken toilet! You have diarrhea of the mouth! So close your mouth and open your ears! Cause when your mouth is open, your ears are closed!"

I would try not to laugh. But Woody was right. I wasn't a good listener.

Young men must learn to listen. And old men must continue to listen.

True, active listening is far too rare in the world today.

Stephen Covey said, "Most people do not listen with the intent to understand; they listen with the intent to reply."

There are few ways to more quickly grow in wisdom, distinguish yourself, and increase your influence and impact on others than by being a person who listens well. Let alone learning to ask good, insightful, follow-up questions from a teachable heart.

Listening is one of those disciplines that is both a skill and a reflection of one's character and humility. Like the character quality of humility, listening isn't ever something you fully, or finally, "master" but something you continually practice and cultivate.

Listening well is one of the primary ways we can demonstrate and communicate

love, care, concern, compassion, wisdom, humility, and respect to those around us.

Listening is powerful.

Listening can save your life and can save others.

Stronger Men learn to listen. To God. To wise counsel. To godly spiritual authority. To your wife, if you're married. To your friends. To your sons and daughters. To those you lead.

Anyone you desire to love well and influence deeply, or even be influenced by, must know and feel that you are listening.

As a young and immature Christian in my early 20s, I was part of a weekly men's group. One week, we had a guest attend who had been a missionary in South America and had suffered the tragic loss of his wife and daughter in a bus accident while taking the gospel to native peoples high in the mountains. It was horribly tragic. It was his worst fear that came to pass.

He shared briefly about his grief and struggles as he wrestled with why God would allow this to happen and how he was endeavoring to move forward in life.

He had walked through deep waters I knew nothing about.

Unfortunately, that didn't stop me from firing away with my passionate advice and "encouragement" and "blah blah blah." I honestly can't even remember what I said. It's embarrassing to think about.

At the end of the night, he handed me a small piece of paper that he had written a note on, at some point, while I was talking and dominating the "group discussion."

It simply said, "*Brother, I appreciate your zeal. Learn to listen.*"

And I believe it had a reference to **Proverbs 10:19**, "*When words are many, sin is not absent, but he who holds his tongue is wise.*"

Or, it could have been, **Proverbs 18:13**, "*He who answers before listening—that is his folly and shame.*"

Or maybe it was **Proverbs 19:20**, which says, "*Listen to advice and accept instruction, and in the end you will be wise.*"

It could have been **Proverbs 23:19**, "*Listen, my son, and be wise, and keep your heart on the right path.*"

You get the point.

And so did I. After a few, humbling moments of reflection.

My initial reaction revealed my default pride, as I recoiled in dismay and started to take offense. After all, I was "on fire for the Lord."

Thankfully, the Holy Spirit convicted me and I knew He had just put His finger on the next critical issue in my character development that needed to be addressed.

He loved me well, graciously but courageously rebuking me, not in front of others, but with a note filled with truth and grace.

To this day, sadly, I can't remember his name and I never saw him again. Yet, in no small way, the Lord used him to change my life and propel me on a needed journey of growth toward becoming a more loving, more humble, more self-aware, and wiser person. Not that I've arrived, by any stretch, but that experience and encounter marked me.

Proverbs 15:31 says, "*He who listens to a life-giving rebuke will be at home among the wise.*"

I can quickly find these Proverbs about listening along with many others in my Bible to this day. They are all highlighted. It's the same Bible I had the night he handed me the note.

Later that same night, I sat in my room and read the entire book of Proverbs in one sitting. I highlighted every use of the word "listen," "pay attention," "listens," "heeds," and everywhere the mouth or ears were mentioned. It's well over 40 references in the 31 chapters of Proverbs.

It changed my life. My family, friends, and I owe that man, and a few others who've been courageous enough to hold me accountable over the years, a debt of gratitude.

While I'm still a work in progress today, if you ask my wife and kids what qualities they most appreciate about me, they often say, "he's a good listener." It blows me away. I shake my head and think, "Well Lord, that's all You. Thank You!"

In our tech-saturated and device-driven world today, the distractions from true listening are more than any time in human history. I know I still have a long way to go to stay on top of wrangling these things under control.

That's an immediate step of action for us men in this endeavor to love well by listening well, to the Lord, and to our families. Brothers, we've got to learn to deal with our phones. Put it away. Create time and space that is tech-less. Look your family in the eye. Talk. Play games. Read. Be creative. Do something active together. Enjoy meals without phones or tech.

As a man, learn to sit quietly with the Lord. Take a walk. Go for a hike or run. Turn off the radio in the car. Or listen to worship music that tunes your mind and heart to the Holy Spirit.

If we are to be Stronger Men who live to please the Lord and love others well, we must be men who can listen.

Dietrich Bonhoeffer, 20th century German pastor and theologian, who was executed by hanging in 1945 for opposing Adolf Hitler, wrote the following about listening in his book, "Life Together," as he describes his experience of Christian community in an underground seminary:

> "There is a kind of listening with half an ear that presumes already to know what the other person has to say. It is an impatient, inattentive listening, that despises the brother and is only waiting for a chance to speak and thus get rid of the other person. This is no fulfillment of our obligation, and it is certain that here too our attitude toward our brother only reflects our relationship to God. It is little wonder that we are no longer capable of the greatest service of listening that God has committed to us, that of hearing our brother's confession, if we refuse to give ear to our brother on lesser subjects. Secular education today is aware that often a person can be helped merely by having someone who will listen to him seriously, and upon this insight it has constructed its own soul therapy, which has attracted great numbers of people, including Christians. But Christians have forgotten that the ministry of listening has been committed to them by Him who is Himself the great listener and whose work they should share. We should listen with the ears of God that we may speak the Word of God."

As a pastor, I regularly hear people unpack their pain, fear, frustration, care, concern, sin, or perspective in a conflict. Whether or not I will be faithful or helpful in those situations entirely depends on my ability to actively listen, both to the person and to the Holy Spirit. It is my desire and prayer to be able to express the love and presence of Jesus to others, to provide wisdom, insight, or encouragement, and to offer compassion and wise counsel from the Word of God.

This is also true in my roles as a husband, father, and friend. And the same is true in your roles and in your field as leaders and workers in the marketplace·

Proverbs 12:18 says, "*Reckless words pierce like a sword, but the tongue of the wise brings healing.*"

I've been on the receiving end of powerful listening and wise and healing words that have changed my life.

What if more men became these kinds of listeners and lovers? How do you think it would impact your marriage? Your relationship with your kids? Your contribution in the marketplace?

Stronger Men get ahold of their tongue and words. They listen carefully and intently, and they speak words that build up, not words that tear down.

To the young men reading this, there's nothing better or wiser that you could do than commit to being a good listener and to develop self-control over your words.

Listen, my son, to your father's instruction and do not forsake your mother's teaching. **Proverbs 1:8**

In our journey of faith, as Stronger Men, let us learn from the example of young Samuel, who became one of the greatest prophets in the Old Testament. As a young boy, he was taught to recognize the calling of God, and in **1 Samuel 3:10** he responded by saying, "*Speak, LORD, for your servant is listening.*"

Let that be our prayer.

As we listen to Him, trust Him, and follow Him, we will become more and more like our true older Brother, the Stronger Man, the Perfect Son, Jesus Christ. He said, "*For I did not speak of My own accord, but the Father who sent Me commanded Me what to say and how to say it. I know that His command leads to eternal life. So whatever I say is just what the Father has told Me to say*" (**John 12:49-50**).

He listened perfectly and He lived perfectly. He succeeded where we fail. Not a word was out of place. And He offers us life-changing grace to follow in His footsteps with the help of the Holy Spirit. Not perfectly, but increasingly.

The Father says to us, about Jesus, "*This is my Son, listen to Him.*"

This is where it must begin. By first being sons who not only hear but who learn to listen carefully to the wisdom of our fathers, spiritual fathers, and above all to our heavenly Father and the Lord Jesus Christ. We must listen carefully to the Word of God. We must learn to distinguish His voice from the voice of the enemy and our flesh. We must not forget our Father's teaching. We must not lean on our own understanding but trust in the Lord with all our heart. We must submit ourselves in humility to Him, fighting our pride, refusing to be wise in our own eyes, as teachable sons, who know we are loved by our Father and who live to honor Him in all we think, say, and do. We must men who speak healing words of life.

What kind of impact would that have on others?

What kind of soldiers, farmers, and athletes might we become if we are first sons who love, listen, trust, speak, and seek to obey our Father, moment by moment?

May we live all our days to bring glory and honor to the One who loved us, listened to our cry for help, forgave us, adopted us, welcomed us in, speaks affirmation over us even now, and calls us to join Him in His redemptive work in the world.

May God be pleased to raise up a generation of these sons, these men. Stronger Men.

LET'S PRAY

Father, teach us to be men who listen. Help us hear Your voice and heed Your voice. Give us ears to hear and the courage to obey as we love those You have given us to protect, provide for, and lead. May all that we do be done in love. May all that we say be filled with truth and grace, in love. May our wives, our children, our friends and those You send our way, experience the presence and love of Jesus in us and through us as we listen and speak with the humility and wisdom that comes from above. Speak to us, Lord, even now. Show us where You want to work in our lives next, what areas need our repentance, our attention, and what You would have us do and say in our most important relationships. Help us to be doers of Your Word, not merely hearers. In Jesus' Name, amen

FROM A STRONGER MAN

He'll never leave me nor forsake me.

My dad was my hero...for the first three years of my life. Although I was young, I can remember bits and pieces of the moment of my parent's divorce. I didn't completely understand what was going on...there were verbal arguments, yelling...never physically violent, but I could sense that my hero was about to leave and I wanted to somehow stop that from happening and my mom from crying.

I am the youngest of eight kids from three different moms. It didn't take long for me to figure out that my parents probably didn't intend to have me, and for 37 years I couldn't shake the nagging voice in my head that told me that my dad left because I was one too many.

I loved my dad even through the brokenness. He would come back to town and into our lives on special occasions, holidays, and some birthdays, and my siblings and I absolutely could not wait for the promised trip to Hawaii and Disneyland that never came.

By God's grace (before I even knew what that was) I was able to get to know my dad on a deeper level when, in my early 20s, he was diagnosed with Parkinson's disease. That diagnosis finally slowed him down and brought him home. I, along with my siblings, were able to help take care of him through the last few years before his death.

This was years before I was saved, so although I'm grateful for that time we spent together—the long conversations we had about his regrets as a father, how I forgave him, and his impending date with death—I only wish I knew the gospel in those days so that I could've pointed my broken hero to Jesus.

Although that thought still brings me to my knees, I trust in the Lord that His ways are higher than mine, and that He ALWAYS works things out for the good of those who love Him and who are called according to His purpose.

And who is to say that in his last moments before his death, God, like the story of the thief on the cross, didn't open my dad's eyes to see that Jesus is who He says He is, and then grant him repentance.

But those details I leave to my heavenly Father who, thanks to Jesus' life, death, and resurrection, I now know will never leave me nor forsake me. And that has changed everything.

Shaun, 45

REFLECT & DISCUSS

1. What is your biggest takeaway from this chapter? What stood out to you most as you read?

_____

_____

_____

2. Why is listening so important? What does it reveal and produce in our relationships? What does listening communicate to others?

_____

_____

_____

3. What is the danger and damage in being a poor listener? How have you seen this truth play out in your life and relationships or in the lives of people around you?

_____

_____

_____

4. How can you actively practice becoming a better listener? How can you lead the members of your family to value listening well and to become better listeners?

_____

_____

_____

5. Multiple Proverbs were cited in the chapter. Which one or two stood out to you the most? Why? How would applying this Proverb to your life make a difference?

_____

_____

_____

6. Why are men in general notorious for being poor listeners? What does this reveal about default pitfalls for men? How should Stronger Men respond?

_____

_____

_____

7. Who is a godly example of a Stronger Man in your life who modeled good listening for you? Where possible, find a way to thank him for that gift and example.

_____

_____

_____

TAKE ACTION

- Memorize one or more of the Proverbs in this chapter. This coming week, reflect on your listening in conversations and practice learning to "W. A. I. T." Which stands for, "Why Am I Talking?" What do you learn or notice when you apply this focus?

- As a family, practice having one single conversation at the dinner table, where everyone listens and only one person talks at a time. This isn't to say that it's never okay to have lively cross-talk at the table. But if you come from a family who always practices the big "free-for-all" with people interrupting and talking over one another, you are likely reinforcing poor listening habits that will need correcting eventually. At some point at the table, bring the chatter to a focus and practice asking good questions and actively listening to each other. How easy or hard is it to implement? What is hard about this? What is good or helpful about it?

WEEK 12

GOD'S DESIGN FOR YOUR FAMILY

Children, obey your parents in the Lord, for this is right. "Honor your father and mother"—which is the first commandment with a promise—"so that it may go well with you and that you may enjoy long life on the earth." Fathers, do not exasperate your children; instead, bring them up in the training and instruction of the Lord.

EPHESIANS 6:1-4

God's design for the family is not a mystery.

But we live in a day and age when man's opinion is constantly challenging or replacing the truth of God's Word. The wreckage is everywhere.

The brokenness of the family is rampant, in large part, due to the failure of men.

It's also true that our family of origin has a massive shaping influence on our lives. Many men have no clue what a godly family should look, sound, or feel like because they've never seen or experienced it firsthand.

Thankfully, God is the Father of all true fatherhood and all healthy family life (Ephesians 3:14), and He is in the business of redeeming men and redeeming families.

Here's a simple summary of God's design for the family:

HUSBANDS/FATHERS Husbands and fathers are to be humble, godly, tough, and tender men who are in the game, actively protecting, providing, leading, and loving their wives and children. They are to be the "pastors" of their family, knowing God's principles and modeling the character of Jesus, as they lead their little flock under the influence and power of the Holy Spirit. They are primarily responsible to ensure their children are trained and educated in the fear and instruction—'paideia'—of the Lord, instilling the character, virtues, and culture of God's Kingdom and a biblical worldview of Truth.

WIVES/MOTHERS Wives and mothers are to be humble, godly, gifted warrior-daughters who are partnering with their husbands in helping, nurturing, teaching, and loving their husbands and children. They are to be the "helpers" of their family, knowing God's principles and modeling the character of Jesus, as they nobly help lead their little flock under the influence and power of the Holy Spirit.

CHILDREN/SIBLINGS Children and siblings are to be humble, godly, respectful, and obedient to their parents and loving, encouraging, and supportive of their siblings. They are to contribute to the order, peace, and discipline of the home by their respectful attitudes, encouraging speech, and responsible behavior. They are to learn God's principles and grow in the character of Jesus, as they come to love Jesus and live under the influence and power of the Holy Spirit.

When a man is in the game, humbly submitted to Jesus, loving and leading his wife, actively teaching and training his kids, the resulting climate and culture of that home and that family is a breath of fresh spiritual, emotional, and relational air to those within and to those around.

It is the man's responsibility to lead and establish this kind of home.

This doesn't mean it's "perfect" or without its challenges. But it does mean it is functioning under the blessing of God's design, and the Spirit of Jesus is reigning over and under that roof as the individual members learn to repent and walk in the power and fruit of the Holy Spirit. (See Galatians 5:22-23.)

The difference is dramatic.

Consider your home environment using the following 20 characteristics. Rate both your family of origin (with an O) and your current family situation (with an X):

Strife   **Peace**

| 0 | 1 | 2 | 3 | 4 | 5 | 6 | 7 | 8 | 9 | 10 |

Criticism   **Encouragement**

| 0 | 1 | 2 | 3 | 4 | 5 | 6 | 7 | 8 | 9 | 10 |

Chaos   **Order**

| 0 | 1 | 2 | 3 | 4 | 5 | 6 | 7 | 8 | 9 | 10 |

Cursing   **Blessing**

| 0 | 1 | 2 | 3 | 4 | 5 | 6 | 7 | 8 | 9 | 10 |

Loneliness   **Love**

| 0 | 1 | 2 | 3 | 4 | 5 | 6 | 7 | 8 | 9 | 10 |

Selfishness   **Servanthood**

| 0 | 1 | 2 | 3 | 4 | 5 | 6 | 7 | 8 | 9 | 10 |

Foolishness   **Wisdom**

| 0 | 1 | 2 | 3 | 4 | 5 | 6 | 7 | 8 | 9 | 10 |

Darkness   **Light**

| 0 | 1 | 2 | 3 | 4 | 5 | 6 | 7 | 8 | 9 | 10 |

Sinful, fleshly attitudes   **The fruit of the Spirit**

| 0 | 1 | 2 | 3 | 4 | 5 | 6 | 7 | 8 | 9 | 10 |

Sharp tongues   **Life-giving speech**

| 0 | 1 | 2 | 3 | 4 | 5 | 6 | 7 | 8 | 9 | 10 |

SON

Unhealthy secrets   **Healthy surprises**

| 0 | 1 | 2 | 3 | 4 | 5 | 6 | 7 | 8 | 9 | 10 |

Danger   **Refuge**

| 0 | 1 | 2 | 3 | 4 | 5 | 6 | 7 | 8 | 9 | 10 |

Isolation   **Hospitality**

| 0 | 1 | 2 | 3 | 4 | 5 | 6 | 7 | 8 | 9 | 10 |

Manipulation/control   **Honor/respect**

| 0 | 1 | 2 | 3 | 4 | 5 | 6 | 7 | 8 | 9 | 10 |

Lies   **Truth**

| 0 | 1 | 2 | 3 | 4 | 5 | 6 | 7 | 8 | 9 | 10 |

Bitterness   **Forgiveness**

| 0 | 1 | 2 | 3 | 4 | 5 | 6 | 7 | 8 | 9 | 10 |

Anger   **Self-control**

| 0 | 1 | 2 | 3 | 4 | 5 | 6 | 7 | 8 | 9 | 10 |

Stinginess/greed   **Generosity**

0   1   2   3   4   5   6   7   8   9   10

Depression/sadness   **Laughter/joy**

0   1   2   3   4   5   6   7   8   9   10

Hypocrisy   **Authentic faith**

0   1   2   3   4   5   6   7   8   9   10

In general, when you total up the numbers, a score of 0-99 is RED, 100-150 is YELLOW, and 151-200 is GREEN.

Any line consistently at a 4 or less would be cause for serious concern and immediate focused attention and correction, including involving godly mentors, short-term pastoral counsel, or even professional counseling from a biblically-based, Christian family counselor.

Any line consistently at a 5-7 should also warrant intentional focus and open conversation within the family to discuss ways to grow in that area.

And lest you are tempted to think that a family who regularly exudes and experiences 8-10 in each area is a unicorn, let me encourage you and challenge you to hear that it is not only possible but totally attainable and is the witness of families being led by Stronger Men under the power of the Holy Spirit.

Even strong families can be lulled to sleep, and any characteristic can start to slip in a day. Therefore, these qualities must be cultivated daily and celebrated regularly.

The right side of those statements is what a truly Spirit-filled home should look, sound, and feel like on a regular basis.

Which makes sense when we remember and believe that God's Word is true, and His design works and bears the fruit of humility and wisdom.

"Wisdom is proved right by her children" **Luke 7:35**. See also Psalm 127 and Psalm 128.

Why would we settle or shoot for anything less?

What kind of family do you want to build?

Where do you need to give the most attention and focus? How will you lead the way?

FOR EVERY SEASON OF MANHOOD

For the young men reading this, the time to decide to become a Stronger Man and prepare to build this kind of healthy, thriving family is now.

153

And for those who have failed in the past, the story is not over. Even if your kids are raised and gone, you still have time to repent of any sin, own your mistakes, acknowledge your shortcomings, and pray for and support your children and grandchildren, and other families, in turning the tide to raise a healthy family under the blessing of the heavenly Father.

God's arm is not too short that He cannot save!

We cannot change the past, but there is always hope for the future. God can still flip the script. He can redeem the lost years, just as He can redeem lost sons and daughters, and He can restore and repair that which is broken down and in disarray.

Whether or not full restoration will be realized on this side of Heaven, God alone knows. But the path of humble confession, earnest prayer, and redeemed ambition is available to every man reading this.

From generation to generation, God is faithful and His promises are true. They are for you and your household. Lead the way!

Stronger Men do not give up.

Stronger Men do not put their heads in the sand.

Stronger Men do not take it for granted or assume it will all be okay with a presumptuous attitude or lethargic non-active response.

We don't shrug our shoulders and hang our heads in shame. Nor do we pass off our responsibility to someone else. Where God brings others alongside to pray, help, and assist, praise God. He has His people all over and can certainly use others who may be in proximity to your kids or grandkids. But He still wants your prayers and efforts in the mix wherever possible.

For those on the front end of building their family, or preparing for that reality in the future, make every effort to lay a solid foundation and build it strong from the start. Get wisdom now! Read, study, ask, observe.

For those in the heat of the battle, currently in the parenting game, it's time to outwit, outplay, and outlast the enemy and any rebellion or spiritual indifference in your home. The time to fight, build, repair, and course correct is NOW!

LINKING ARMS AND LEADING THE WAY

Stronger Men link arms with healthy churches to build healthy families. So find a church where the Bible is plainly taught and where men are encouraged to be the strong, humble, Spirit-filled leaders in their homes. Then get involved.

Men, it is our responsibility to ensure our homes are in order. It is not something you can ignore or pass off without serious consequences. But we don't go it alone. We band together with like-minded men and support each other in the task.

Imagine a family, a church, and even a society where this is the norm?

Imagine a family of multiple generations who are walking together in this kind of family fruit and life-giving relationship?

Imagine family gatherings, holidays, and reunions being anticipated with joy instead of dread? With healthy memories instead of embarrassing scenes?

It takes clear vision, deep conviction, and steadfast courage to steer your family ship into these calm and refreshing waters. And when it's going off course, it's your job to step into the fray and bring order to the chaos, function to the dysfunction, boundaries to the bozos, responsibility to the unruly, and righteousness and peace to the frat party and cat fights.

And when you're not in a position to bring change to a dysfunctional family situation, a Stronger Man refuses to be manipulated, controlled, guilted, or shamed into subjecting his family to unhealthy environments that tolerate toxicity. We draw the boundaries necessary to protect our own family and we build a home of peace, where the values of the Kingdom of God set the tone and where there is spiritual safety and security for hearts young and old alike.

Whether there was honor in your family of origin or not, whether there were godly examples or not, Stronger Men do not live with a victim mentality or helpless attitude. They run to the Father for healing, they study His Word for His principles, they seek out spiritually fruitful families for wisdom, they commit to God's design, they lock arms with brothers in the fight, and they lead the way to build a brighter future for their family.

But as for me and my house, we will serve the LORD. **Joshua 24:15**

Unless the LORD builds the house, its builders labor in vain.
Psalm 127:1

LET'S PRAY

Father, You are the Father of fathers and the true Builder of families. Thank You for the truth of Your word, Your promises to bless those who walk in Your ways, and Your presence with us every step along the way. Thank You for not leaving us in the dark. Help every man reading this to have a clear vision of the kind of man, husband, father, brother, son, and leader You are calling him to be in the arena of our families. Give encouragement where needed, challenge where needed, healing where needed, hope where needed, and wisdom and courage to begin to take action and move forward today. Fill my brother reading this with Your Holy Spirit, and show him his next step. In Jesus' Name, amen.

FROM A STRONGER MAN

I was born into a traditional family, but grew up living mostly homeless. My father was never able to hold a job for very long and as early as I can remember my family would be kicked out of trailers, apartments, and family "friends" homes after overstaying our welcome. At various times we would find ourselves squatting without electricity or working plumbing. We eventually landed in local homeless shelters.

As I grew older, I found myself repeating the same mistakes of my father, as well as making many of my own. This included drug use, apartment evictions, and living out of my car to name a few. Eventually I found myself sitting in a holding cell for DWI. I was spiraling and my sin was controlling my life. At the age of 21 my father died. With this, I decided to "clean up my act." Within a few short months, I ended up taking in my 6-year-old sister and getting married to a coworker. I was trying to fix things my way, and on the surface it looked like things were finally changing. However, having never learned how to lead, or what a marriage should look like, I would find myself divorced, raising two children on my own, broken, and desperate.

Eventually, I found myself working for a strong, God-fearing man who extended the invitation to come to church on multiple occasions. Finally accepting, I was quickly surrounded by some amazing men with a heart for Christ. In that church, God rescued me out of the despair of my sin. I learned how powerful and mighty His forgiveness is, and what a loving Father looked like. On April 8th of 2012, I chose to follow Christ and was baptized. God has been flipping the script on my life ever since.

I attended the Stronger Man Nation Conference, and in the final hours of the conference, the messaging shifted towards father wounds. I remember thinking, "Father wounds? I don't have any father wounds. My father loved me. This message is for everyone else." However, hearing this message, I began to realize that I had been holding onto anger and bitterness towards my father because of the way that I grew up. What also dawned on me was that, until God had saved me, I had repeated the same mistakes of my father.

Upon leaving the conference, the men were called to do one of three things when we left that day. Thank their father for being a good father, if they had one. Forgive their earthly father for the wounds they had received. Ask their father for forgiveness for their rebellious behavior. I felt an overwhelming conviction—one that I can only say came from the Holy Spirit— all the while not exactly knowing what I was actually about to do. I knew where I needed to go. My fathers grave.

How can you forgive a man who has been dead for 15 years? For me, it came down to another name shared on this tombstone: my grandfather's. **A swell of grief consumed me. In tears and on my knees, I prayed. I was able to extend forgiveness to my deceased father and released this anger I didn't know I had. I realized that he was also suffering from a father wound. For many years my father had tried to live up to the expectations of an abusive and overbearing father who he could never please. Eventually giving up and letting everything slide. This poured out into all areas of his life. This gave way to the inability to provide for his family and never requiring accountability or setting standards for his own son's to live by. This father wound became a legacy. A legacy that I had lived until my heavenly Father had rescued me.**

God has become everything my earthly father couldn't be and has changed my heart, thoughts, and desires for life. Since following Christ, I have witnessed an incredible amount of grace in my life, and God continues to pour it out on me in overwhelming ways. God, being the good Father He is, has loved me enough to ensure I don't stay comfortable where I am at in my walk or my sin. As such, following Christ has not always been easy, but it has always been worth it. Today, I am leading in a marriage of eight years with my bride, where God is our foundation. Where once I was homeless, I am now a homeowner. Where my father couldn't hold a job, and handouts were often required, now my heavenly Father has provided a business that allows me to use my resources to give back and help feed people who are living in similar situations that I grew up in. God is creating a new legacy in the next generation of my family. I have been granted the responsibility of raising four children. One of them being my sister, who recently graduated from college debt free and has started a new family with her new God-fearing husband. My now teenager started working in my business last year at the age of 12. One just started homeschooling, and the youngest will join her when she gets older. Each one of them is learning that, where I fall short as their dad, God is the perfect Father, and that I trust Him, and they can too.

Stephen, 38

REFLECT & DISCUSS

1. What is your biggest takeaway from this chapter? What stood out to you as you read?

_____

_____

_____

2. Share the score for your family of origin in the 20 characteristic assessment. Share the score for your current family. What are your thoughts and feelings about those scores? Was the assessment helpful or hard?

_____

_____

_____

3. What are the next steps for you to grow/improve your current family health in these characteristics? Where do you need to give the most attention and focus?

_____

_____

_____

4. In the simple summary of God's design for the family at the beginning of the chapter, what stands out to you the most? What questions does it bring up, if any? What would you add?

_____

_____

_____

5. What kinds of experiences have you had with regard to drawing boundaries in order to protect and lead your family away from unhealthy or dysfunctional dynamics?

_____

_____

_____

6. What gives you hope when you think about the future of your family and family relationships? What would you like to see the Lord do?

_____

_____

_____

7. How can you contribute to the strength of other men and families around you? How can you help build a healthy, family-strengthening community that is a bright witness and example to the beauty of God's design for the family? What would that look like?

_____

_____

_____

_____

TAKE ACTION

- Review the assessment in this chapter with your wife (if married), and have her assess her family of origin. Have an honest, grace-filled conversation about the strengths and weaknesses of your two families. Give each other permission to speak freely without attacking each other or getting defensive. The goal is not to nitpick either family but to honestly assess your experience and then commit to a shared vision for growth and health moving forward. Talk about the kind of family environment you want to create and how you can partner together to build it. If you're a young man or single, share and discuss the assessment with a close friend.

- Repent of any areas where you have contributed to unhealthy habits or patterns and commit to intentional growth in that area with the Lord's help and the help of your wife/family.

ADDITIONAL QUESTIONS FOR DISCUSSION

1. How would you describe your hometown where you grew up?

2. What are some fun childhood memories that come to mind?

3. What were holidays and birthdays like in your home growing up?

4. What's one of the dumbest things you did as a young man?

5. What's the biggest compliment you've ever received?

6. What do you consider your greatest accomplishment in life so far?

7. If you had siblings, what was your relationship like with your siblings growing up? What is it like today?

8. In what ways would you want to emulate attributes and qualities of manhood from your father?

9. In what ways would you NOT want to emulate attributes and qualities of manhood from your father?

10. How would you describe the kind of legacy you want to leave? What words do you hope others use to describe your impact?

11. What is your definition for "success?" What does it mean to be a "successful man?"

12. Share a version of your spiritual history and journey.

13. What were your first experiences of church like?

14. What would you say is currently the biggest hurdle or obstacle in the growth of your faith and relationship with God?

15. What weighs on your mind/heart the most these days?

16. What changes are needed in your current family routine (daily, weekly, monthly)?

17. What do you do for fun? What do you do with your family for fun?

18. Are you satisfied with your current level of availability and connection with your wife and kids? With your dad? With your mom? What would improve these relationships?

19. Are you satisfied with your current relationship with God? What would improve it?

20. If you could talk to your 18-year-old self, what would you say? What counsel/advice would you give yourself? To a young man reading this, what advice would you give yourself 2 years ago?

PRACTICAL WAYS TO LEAN INTO BEING A FREE SON AND A LOVING, STRONGER MAN

- Commit to reading God's Word on a regular basis. The Word of God was written to instruct, encourage, and point you to Jesus. Jesus wants to bring you to the Father and reinforce your true identity as a loved son. There's no replacement for the Word of God in your life. Some men are helped by listening to it audibly through an app like the YouVersion Bible app. There are daily verses and reading plans to help you get started.

- Learn to spend time in prayer. Many men are helped by learning to pray out loud when alone; it has a way of focusing your attention and engages more of your whole person. Prayer can be like a muscle—the only way it gets stronger is through discipline, repetition, and use. Don't give up.

- Practice the discipline of journaling your thoughts, prayers, insights, and life lessons. A journal and the discipline of writing can help you process thoughts and emotions that are inside of you that are often difficult for men to understand or express. Writing forces the mind to focus and articulate a complete and specific thought or idea.

- Listen to worship music that stirs your affections for God and reinforces powerful gospel truth about our identity and freedom in Christ.

- Cultivate the ability to use words to build up others and express emotion and affection to family and loved ones. If you tend to be quieter, challenge yourself to speak up more often, especially in your closest relationships. If you tend to be a talker, challenge yourself to ask more questions and listen more intently.

- Grow in your ability to actively listen and ask good questions.

- Develop your EQ not just your IQ. Emotional intelligence is a relational super power. Relationships are the goal more than just knowledge or information.

- Give more hugs. Express appropriate physical touch, especially with your family.

- Ask those closest to you how they perceive you relationally and emotionally. Are you open or closed? Are you warm or cold? Are you relaxed or tense? Are you calm or intense? Are you approachable or argumentative? Honestly listen to their answers and let them know of your desire to become a more tender, loving man in your closest relationships.

- If you are a father of young kids, wrestle with your kids. Play. Interact. Get down on the floor. Connect with their interests.

- Write notes of encouragement, affirmation, and blessing to your family and friends.

- Let your family see you cry and express honest emotions.

- Make meaningful eye contact.

- Process any unresolved pain, anger, sin, addictions, and struggles. Have you honestly faced the hard stuff in your story? If needed, get help from a Christian counselor to pursue healing.

- Confess all known sin. Sin rots the bones and impacts our spiritual, physical, emotional, and relational freedom. The Bible calls us to confess our sin to a trusted fellow brother in Christ that we might be healed.

- Extend and receive forgiveness where needed. Issues of bitterness and unforgiveness cut off the flow of God's grace in our lives and relationships. They are a key tactic of demonic forces to bind and enslave people.

www.ingramcontent.com/pod-product-compliance
Lightning Source LLC
Chambersburg PA
CBHW051835090426
42736CB00011B/1821